FIGHTING FOR NOW

Fighting for NOW

DIVERSITY AND DISCORD IN THE NATIONAL ORGANIZATION FOR WOMEN

Kelsy Kretschmer

University of Minnesota Press

Minneapolis

London

Published by the University of Minnesota Press
111 Third Avenue South, Suite 290
Minneapolis, MN 55401-2520
http://www.upress.umn.edu

Printed in the United States of America on acid-free paper

The University of Minnesota is an equal-opportunity educator and employer.

Library of Congress Cataloging-in-Publication Data
Names: Kretschmer, Kelsy, author.
Title: Fighting for NOW : diversity and discord in the National Organization for Women / Kelsy Kretschmer.
Description: Minneapolis : University of Minnesota Press, [2019] | Includes bibliographical references and index. |
Identifiers: LCCN 2018020499 (print) | ISBN 978-1-5179-0315-2 (hc) | ISBN 978-1-5179-0316-9 (pb)
Subjects: LCSH: National Organization for Women. | Feminism—United States—History. | Women's rights—United States—History. | Women—Political activity—United States—History.
Classification: LCC HQ1421 .K74 2019 (print) | DDC 320.082/0973—dc23
LC record available at https://lccn.loc.gov/2018020499

UMP BmB

For Christopher, Calvin, and Parker

CONTENTS

ACKNOWLEDGMENTS

This book has taken a long time to write and, in the process, I have accumulated debts all over town, so to speak. The largest share of my debt goes to David S. Meyer, who is the kind of mentor everyone should have. He cared as much about this book as I did, and I am deeply grateful for his guidance and patience as I plodded along. In addition to David, I was lucky to work with a prolific group of scholars at the University of California, Irvine who shaped many of the ideas in this book. Francesca Polletta, Edwin Amenta, and Judith Stepan-Norris, as far as I am concerned, rounded out the world's best and kindest doctoral committee. They guided me toward the better ideas that came out of my dissertation and continued to be important sounding boards as the book developed. I am also grateful to David Snow, Calvin Morrill, Su Yang, and Belinda Robnett for feedback they provided in both formal and informal settings. Parts of *Fighting for NOW* were first workshopped in the Social Movement/Social Justice (SMSJ) Workgroup at UCI, organized by David S. Meyer. I am very grateful to the SMSJ community for helping me become a better scholar.

In collecting data for this research, the special collections staff at the Schlesinger Library and the Sophia Smith Collection were helpful and kind. I left these libraries convinced that archive reading rooms were the best place on earth. The National Organization for Women was generous in allowing me access to its document collections at Schlesinger, and without that access this book would not have been possible. The Kerrissey family housed me while I was visiting the archives in Cambridge and Northampton, Massachusetts, and without their generosity I could not have afforded to collect the critical data for this project. Interviewing activists was a wonderful and illuminating experience, and I am so grateful to the women who took time to talk with me about their lives and work. A variety of institutions and organizations over the years provided crucial financial support. These include the University of California, Irvine Center for Organizational Research (COR); Southern Illinois University, Carbondale; and Oregon State University.

I'm also deeply appreciative of the colleagues who took the time to read and comment on my book proposal and some very rough chapter drafts. This group includes Kristen Barber, Catherine Corrigall Brown, William F. Danaher, Bob Edwards, John McCarthy, Jo Reger, Meghann Pytka, Daisy Verduzco Reyes, Darren Sherkat, Suzanne Staggenborg, and Natasha Zaretsky. During a difficult year in Boston, while I was looking for a job, William A. Gamson and Charlotte Ryan welcomed me into their Media Research and Action Project (MRAP) group at Boston College. I am grateful for their hospitality and intellectual rigor. Jason Weidemann at the University of Minnesota Press has been a patient and enthusiastic supporter of this book. Through early chapter drafts and reviews, he took time to clarify the opaque book publishing process. Even after a few missed deadlines, he remained invested and excited about how this project might inform current feminist debates. I am deeply grateful for his help and guidance.

I benefited from coming into academia with a core group of colleagues who have become dear friends. Even when they did not know what this project was about, they remembered to ask how my book was coming along and to encourage me to get back to it. Their energy and tenacity are endlessly inspiring. My deepest thanks to Kristen Barber, Catherine Corrigall-Brown, Steven A. Boutcher, Daisy Verduzco Reyes, Karen Robinson, and Leah Ruppanner.

My family served as consistent cheerleaders throughout this process. I want nothing more than for this book to make them proud. Thank you to Robert Kretschmer, Rebecca and Scott Wilson, Timothy Stout, Vanessa Stout, Kandi and David Nafziger, Karah and Scott Young, and Riley Kretschmer. Theresa Stout's love and labor for my family made it possible for me to finish the final draft of this book. I am so grateful for all she has done. I was lucky to find a partner in Christopher Stout who engaged with these ideas, encouraged me to write through it when I was in the weeds, and always carved out extra writing time for me. I would not have finished it without his support. Finally, Calvin and Parker Stout were the two cutest motivators I could have asked for. Parker generously waited to be born until the first full draft of this manuscript was submitted. They both helped me learn to work consistently, even when tired, and to get up from the computer every once in a while. They will probably never read this book, but thinking that they might motivated me to finish it.

ORGANIZATION ABBREVIATIONS

BWOA   Black Women Organized for Action
CFC   Catholics for a [Free] Choice
FFL   Feminists for Life
HRW   Human Rights for Women
JCO   Joint Committee of Organizations Concerned with the Status of
Women in the Church
LDEF   NOW Legal Defense and Education Fund
NOW   National Organization for Women
NWL   National Women's Liberation
NWPC   National Women's Political Caucus
OWL   Older Women's League
WEAL   Women's Equity Action League

CHAPTER ONE

Feminist Organizations

Stability versus Creativity?

On November 8, 2016, Donald J. Trump was elected to be the forty-fifth president of the United States, defeating Hillary Rodham Clinton, the first female candidate to be elected by a major party. Clinton had been projected to win in almost every national poll in the months leading up to election night, and she did, in fact, win the popular vote by nearly three million votes. Trump's blatant misogyny, racism, and antipathy toward progressive movements made his election unthinkable to most liberals. The election night results were stunning, and many on the left, particularly those identifying with the feminist movement, went to bed wondering how to respond to such a devastating and surprising outcome.

The unwelcome election outcome has unleashed a new wave of feminist activism—a movement that had been labeled stagnant, if not dead, for decades (Reger 2012). Women, as well as many men, are finding renewed interest in organizing within traditional political channels and in participating in extra-institutional politics like social movement organizations and protest events. Following the election, a group of women scattered across the country began to plan a Women's March to be held on the weekend of Trump's inauguration. There was an outpouring of support for the idea, with tens of thousands of people across the country pledging their attendance within the first few days. By any measure, the March was a smashing success, breaking the record for the largest protest event in the nation's history and drawing roughly four million people into the nation's streets.

Yet internal conflicts in the renewed feminist movement have also emerged. Critics were quick to denounce the March as an exercise in "white feminism," arguing that the sudden willingness of white women to protest only after Clinton's defeat was suspect—where had they been, for example, during the years of Black Lives Matter protests before the election (Stockman 2017)? Other disputes cropped up as well. Trans women felt excluded by the lack of trans speakers and by the many vulva costumes, signs referencing powerful or vindictive vaginas, and ubiquitous "pussy hats"—pink knitted beanies with cat ears, worn as a callout to Trump's boast that he could grab women "by the pussy" whenever he wanted (Greer 2017). Disability rights activists were angry that they were initially excluded from the Women's March platform statement (Ladau 2017) and felt slighted by both the physical layout of the Washington, D.C., event and the lack of representation for disabled women among speakers onstage (Bonde and Bonde 2017).

The Women's March offers a microcosm of the broader feminist movement. While the fights over identity and inclusion may seem like manifestations of a new focus on intersectionality, these same fights have been happening in American feminism for decades. Conflict is a given in any social movement because activists must collaboratively decide on a (one hopes) coherent set of frames and messages—specific enough to be powerful and locally meaningful while also general enough to include a wide range of experiences (Ghaziani 2008). These decisions are always fraught because they are fundamentally about setting boundaries. Any specific demand movement actors assert inevitably leaves out someone's needs and experiences.

A pressing question for all movement leaders and participants is how to manage the inevitable conflict in ways that give space to marginalized members, while not tipping over into tiny, isolated fragments. These fights are at the root of movement factionalism, both between and within organizations. Over time, organizations bear the marks of their boundary conflicts. Sometimes they adjust their structure to include more identities and issues. Sometimes they choose instead to split apart, with groups of members going their own way to build new, autonomous spaces.

Women's March organizers responded to each of these conflicts, and many others, by apologizing and expanding the group's boundaries to include more voices and a broader set of priorities. Other problems were organizational, like the long delay in getting permits for the event, planning the route, creating security and safety plans, and arranging for bathrooms. In the era of Facebook and Twitter, organizing social movement events seems rather easy—within a few days of floating the idea of the March, the original organizers were able to marshal tens of thousands of supporters and hundreds of volunteers. But the challenges they faced in pulling together the event—representing the wide spread of identities and voices and the logistics that needed to be coordinated and paid for—make the need for experienced organizers and organizations abundantly clear.

In the burst of excitement, creativity, and conflict in the planning phases of the March, traditional bureaucratic women's and feminist organizations were largely absent. Even when organizers miscalculated their efforts and caused offense, their grassroots, collectivist approach was celebrated as emerging from and representing a groundswell of authentic feminist outrage. Large bureaucratic feminist groups, on the other end of the organizing spectrum, were criticized as conservative and narrowly focused on their organizational images. In the chaotic lead-up to the March, *Slate* writer Christina Cauterucci (2016) wrote that "big-league" reproductive rights and gender-justice organizations should have been leading the charge following the election but hesitated to sign on to an event they could not control with a message they could not shape. Eventually, overwhelmed by the scope of pulling together a national protest event, Women's March organizers reached out to a broader circle of leaders and established groups to help pull the event together, including the better-known bureaucratic women's organizations like the National Organization for Women (NOW) and Planned Parenthood.

Formalized and bureaucratic groups have a clear advantage in coordinating large events like the Women's March. Groups like NOW and Planned Parenthood have a long history of sponsoring and organizing these events. In 2004, NOW, along with NARAL Pro-Choice America, the Feminist Majority Foundation, and Planned Parenthood, among others, planned and sponsored the March for Women's Lives, with between five hundred thousand and eight hundred thousand participants (organizers' estimates of the turnout were much higher, at 1.5 million) ("Abortion Activists on the March"). Calling on its bureaucratic proficiency and experience, Women's March organizers brought Planned Parenthood in to serve as a "premier partner," focusing on online promotion, coordinating volunteers and staff, and developing security protocols (Kahn 2017). If the Women's March was the exciting cutting edge of the movement, its bureaucratic partners represented movement stability and experience.

Creative Collectives and Boring Bureaucracies?

Within social movements, *how* activists organize matters as much to them as the goals they are working toward. Groups might adopt a wide variety of structures, but the choice frequently boils down to whether activists will formalize and bureaucratize their structures or if they will maintain informal collectives. Activists and scholars alike have argued that the ideal type of feminist structure is closer to the latter: nonbureaucratic, nonhierarchical, participatory, with democratic decision-making (Atkinson 1974; Ferree and Hess 2000; Rothschild-Whitt 1979; Staggenborg 1991). The Women's March, and the group that pulled it off, embraced this form. Bob Bland, co-chair for the March and the continuing organization, describes its structure as collectivist in nature—"an organic, grassroots effort that prides itself on being inclusive, intersectional, and nonhierarchical," with "a horizontal approach to leadership" (Felsenthal 2017). In deploying this rhetoric, the Women's March pulled from a long history of feminist concern about how organizational structures match with movement values.

Activists organize in collectivist ways for many reasons, including a desire to reimagine power relationships and enact radical egalitarianism in their communities. Scholars have also argued that collectives are better able to adapt quickly to new circumstances, allowing them to capitalize on new opportunities for mobilization (Gerlach and Hine 1970; Piven and Cloward 1977; cf. Blee 2012). Unencumbered by elaborate rules for making decisions, they are better able to "engage in disruptive action" that might be vetoed in more formal organizations (Caniglia and Carmin 2005; Tarrow 1998). They are often explicitly contrasted to bureaucratic organizations in this regard.

Collectivist forms are also chosen for moral reasons, when activists want to avoid becoming "empty bureaucratic institution(s) instead of . . . vehicle[s] for change" (Fitzgerald and Rodgers 2000, 579). In this framing of organizational structures, bureaucracies redirect activist energy for social change to organizational maintenance, robbing movements of energy and ingenuity (Piven and Cloward 1977). Rather than generating new forms of resistance and strategy, activists are made into constituents, voting for leaders and policies, and pumped for money to support the organization—a dark view of bureaucratic organizations, indeed.

NOW provides an excellent theoretical puzzle challenging this common assertion. Despite bureaucratic groups' dull reputation as focused on routine organizational maintenance, NOW has experienced countless rounds of infighting and factionalism. It has split dozens of times when groups of members have defected to build independent groups. Members have left over a wide range of issues, including abortion, lesbian rights, the Equal Rights Amendment (ERA), participation in mainstream politics, racial representation, and structural disagreements. In fact, NOW's long history of splitting demonstrates how its bureaucratic form actually created the pathways through which many new feminist groups formed. How do we balance NOW's history of organizational splitting with its undeniable durability over decades of turbulent political and cultural contexts?

An examination of NOW between 1966 and 2009 allows us to challenge our taken-for-granted assumptions about bureaucratic movement organizations. There is no denying the historical record that feminism's formalized groups lasted longer than the smaller collectives. Yet our static distinction between organizational forms overestimates bureaucracies' internal unity, while underestimating their potential as creative engines in their social movements. I argue for a new perspective of bureaucratic groups in two ways.

First, though bureaucratic structures provide myriad organizational benefits, they do not inherently prevent schisms. Instead, formalization allows NOW, and groups like it, effectively to weather consistently erupting internal conflicts. In other words, NOW experienced a wide range of factionalism over its life-span, but because it survived these episodes, we have largely failed to recognize those conflicts as schisms. Our focus on NOW's bureaucratic stability has made us blind to the sheer number of new groups that have emerged from its episodic factionalism.

In fact, its bureaucratic structure often created the very divisions among members that eventually led to organizational splits. Formalization meant clustering members into particular and localized groups, which were often isolated from and very different than members in other parts of the organization. This structure allows bureaucratic organizations to grow large, with expansive agendas and broad memberships. It also incubates factions by bringing diverse kinds of activists under a single organizational roof, while providing them enough autonomy to develop distinct ideologies, strategies, goals, and tactics. Over time, this structure pulls together potent ingredients, combining to produce factionalism and schism.

Second, and related, NOW's staid reputation belies a long history of roiling conflict and internal fights among its members over how to be feminist. Just as with the smaller, flat collectives, NOW's internal conflict was a force for creative generation of new identities and ideologies, which frequently spilled out of NOW's boundaries into the broader movement. This represents an important gap in our understanding of the feminist movement. When we ignore the fights within NOW, including when it was unable or unwilling to contain its internal conflicts, we also fail to see the many ways those fights changed the broader feminist movement. From its inception, NOW was plagued by many of the same fights the smaller groups experienced. Over the past half-century, it has endured factionalism over all of the same issues, and more, that threatened the Women's March. Although NOW survived these battles, its organizational identity and structure were marked, scarred, and transformed in these fights. So, too, was the broader movement, as NOW's splits transformed into innovative organizations and ideological spaces for new kinds of activists (Ryan 1992; Kretschmer 2009, 2014).

It is a critical mistake to see only NOW's dogged durability while turning a blind eye to its history of creative and productive internal battles. The central purpose of this book, then, is to explore and challenge our commonly accepted notions of how bureaucratic organizations like NOW operate in social movements, with particular attention to the ways infighting, factionalism, and organizational splitting are shaped by bureaucratic structures.

Conflict and Breaking Away

Scholars have defined and conceptualized internal conflict in different ways. Generally, infighting is considered to be an early stage in the conflict process, with groups of members struggling with each other over their collective identity and what they represent. Amin Ghaziani (2008) argues that this is unavoidable but healthy conflict, necessary for groups to concretize their shared culture. In contrast to infighting, factions, splits, and schisms are lumped together as evidence of unhealthy conflict and group failure inability to manage differences. From this view, when members leave their organization, it means that the group is fundamentally broken and failing, as signaled by "the proper breakup of the group" (Ghaziani 2008, 12). This is a damning view of organizational splits, and it does not take a deep dive into the social movement literature to find examples of bitter schisms that look very much like simple organizational failure (Balser 1997; Echols 1989; Gamson 1990).

But this view of organizational splitting is incomplete. It neglects the ways conflict and factionalism can produce new organizations without killing the original organization. NOW has remained the largest and best-known feminist organization in the United States, despite its many episodes of schism. Moreover, the perspective that schism is inherently deadly also neglects the reality that many organizational splits are relatively conflict free, with members and leaders recognizing that they are simply better off by splitting some members or functions into new organizations. This happens when groups of members leave to form more narrowly constructed identity groups or when organizations spin off new groups that take advantage of nonprofit tax policies. Importantly, the view that all splits are inherently contentious and fatal does not leave room for the possibility that breakaway organizations can be a sign of innovation and creativity generated by an organization's functioning structure.

I argue that we should take a broader view of organizational splitting, including the possibility that it can be a healthy outcome for individual groups and social movements, by incorporating the language organizational scholars have used to understand breakaway organizations. In that literature, breakaway organizations are defined as new groups created by founders who worked together in a previous group, which served as an incubator in the same industry or movement. Founders' plans for the new organization are "based on ideas developed in the founders' previous organization" (Dyck and Starke 1999, 793; see also Cooper and Gascon 1992). This definition leaves room for conflict in the decision to split away, but it does not *rely* on conflict or group failure to understand how new organizations emerge from existing ones. It also allows us to recognize the generative and creative outcomes of infighting, while recognizing that these benefits can manifest in the creation of new organizations rather than reconciliation in the original group. Sometimes members are inspired by their experiences, both good and bad, in previous organizations, to create something new. From this perspective, a broader view of breakaway organizations includes member defection and the creation of new groups without assuming that their very occurrence is evidence of failure.

This is a truer representation of the complicated character of organizational splitting in social movement industries, which so often requires coalition building and collaboration toward common goals (Zald and McCarthy 1980). Schisms are utterly common, often involving intense internal factionalism and conflict. But even a conflicted beginning does not preclude a working, functional relationship between the resulting organizations after a split. Because they continue to share a broader movement and many of the same overarching goals, breakaway organizations have an interest in moving beyond prior conflicts to build new, cooperative relationships. The cases presented in this book are a testament to this preference.

Building from a neutral view of organizational splitting, I argue that, while conflict and factionalism are inevitable in social movements, the trajectory of factionalism and the outcomes afterward are deeply shaped by the organizational structures in which that conflict occurs (Zald and

Berger 1978). In more structurally complicated organizations like NOW, there is not just one pathway by which groups factionalize and choose to break away. Instead, NOW—a national organization with a federated and segmented structure—is decentralized, with most members organized into smaller units that enjoy immense freedom and autonomy in choosing how to be feminist. In designing these structures, leaders consciously created a variety of spaces for members to find each other and to develop niche collective identities reflecting their specific and localized ideas about feminism. In these smaller spaces within NOW, members experimented with many different tactics, ideologies, and organizational forms only loosely governed by NOW's top-level, national administration.

These smaller units of NOW, including its chapters, task forces, committees, and satellite organizations, have been sites of enormous creativity and innovation for the feminist movement. At the same time, these smaller units are often very different from each other, with each shaped by its local culture, community, and network. This can mean members in one part of NOW embody very different feminist identities than those in other NOW locations. Most of the time, even very different members can find ways to coexist without boiling over into conflict and factionalism (Reger 2002b). At other times, and under specific circumstances, bringing so many competing identities and ideologies under one organizational umbrella produces conflict and factionalism that ends in organizational splitting.

Moreover, even as they enjoy freedom to experiment and innovate within their localized groups, members must still navigate the challenges of membership in a large, national organization. Leaders at the national level experience their own needs and identity strains as they seek to represent thousands of diverse members with a unified agenda and strategy for achieving goals. National leaders are also responsible for organizational maintenance and continuity—needs that can sometimes require prioritizing goals in ways that rankle local members. Even when they enjoy freedom in their local spaces to be feminist in the ways that are most meaningful to them, members may drift so far from the collective NOW identity represented by national leaders that they can no longer justify continuing to be members. Local members may choose to split away to form something that better represents their vision of feminist progress. Professionalized national leaders also intentionally split off new organizations to engage in different kinds of work, such as legal advocacy or education work. In both scenarios, splitting the main organization into smaller groups is often a way to *reduce* conflict, allowing newly distinct groups to focus on the activities, identities, and tactics they care about most and for which they are best designed.

In the remainder of this chapter, I present an overview of NOW's history and structure. I then describe the data I use to understand the process of NOW's organizational splitting. Finally, I offer a brief explanation of the organization of the book, presenting a short synopsis of each chapter.

The National Organization for Women

NOW's formation in 1966 was itself a kind of schism, when members of the President's Commission on the Status of Women (PCSW) grew frustrated by the lack of progress in dealing with women's continuing discrimination and inequality in the public realm. The President's Commission was formed in 1961 by executive order, as a compromise struck by President John Kennedy, who felt pressure to respond to discrimination against women while not alienating labor groups by supporting the ERA. As a part of this order, state-level commissions were also formed and met annually in Washington, D.C. Around the time of the 1966 state meeting, some commission members, government workers, and other activists began to voice their frustration at the lack of progress being made by the Equal Employment Opportunity Commission (EEOC) to enforce Title VII of the 1964 Civil Rights Act barring sex discrimination. Many contacted Betty Friedan, serving as the face of contemporary feminism after publishing her landmark book *The Feminine Mystique*. In the months leading up to the meeting, a network of underground feminists working within the state bureaucracy coaxed Friedan, trying to convince her to publicly demand that the state commissions hold the EEOC accountable for its obstruction and that it enforce the law (Friedan 2000).

Attending the conference on a press pass arranged by Catherine East, a consummate Washington insider employed on the PCSW, Friedan used her hotel room to host a meeting of about fifteen women to assess their options for improving the situation. More comfortable working within the system, the group decided that they would present a resolution that "demanded enforcement of Title VII and called for Richard Graham's reappointment" (Davis 1999, 54). Graham was one of the four male EEOC commissioners and the only one who had proved willing to support Title VII, and his term was nearly up. Graham, incidentally, had been actively trying to convince East that women would need to organize an independent pressure group to force the EEOC's hand on women's discrimination. When the group attempted to present their resolution the following day, Esther Peterson, vice chair of the PCSW, informed the group that no resolutions were being accepted. Finding their path blocked, the group began to plan their new activist organization over lunch. They settled on the name "National Organization for Women," and by the end of the day, twenty-seven women had joined, each contributing five dollars (Banaszak 2010; Davis 1999).

NOW founders set to work organizing a national conference in October 1966. By that time, the membership had swelled to three hundred, with roughly thirty attending the conference in Washington, D.C. The members formally adopted NOW's statement of purpose, including its vow to fight job and wage discrimination, educational inequality, political inequality, and the "false image" of women's representation in the media, among other issues (Friedan 2000, 177). The group also established a basic structure, with a president, a board of directors, a variety of task forces, and self-directed local chapters. The task force structure included committees devoted to each of the concerns addressed in NOW's statement of purpose and would eventually grow to include a wide variety of other issues. Maren Lockwood Carden (1974), one of the first scholars to evaluate the reach of the feminist movement, believed that NOW would survive in the long run because of its bureaucratic structure, generalist objectives, and diverse interests.

At annual conferences, members would set policy, which would be carried out by national officers and the board of directors in between. Given that so many of the founders' careers had been in government, law, business, and media, their attentions were often geared toward political institutions and large corporations. Their status helped them achieve early policy wins—the EEOC finally held hearings on Title VII, which it had been so reluctant to enforce. President Johnson signed Executive Order 11375, which barred federal contractors from engaging in sex discrimination. The Civil Service Commission began to show serious signs of recruiting and hiring women for top positions (Davis 1999). At the local level, chapters were developing rapidly across the country. New recruits were invited to join national task forces and to engage in local actions in their own communities in NOW's name.

As NOW emerged the face of liberal feminism, it focused on "[changing] society so that women's status, treatment, opportunities, and condition in life are improved" (Martin 1990, 193). Its particular brand of feminism came to represent the movement's ideological center and new recruits flocked to the organization. This gave the young organization enormous weight in conversations among activists across the movement, and with the broader public, who viewed NOW as the movement's representative. Its early prominence also made the organization a target for wrath from all sides. NOW's national level operated mostly as a liberal reform group, while its local chapters ran the spectrum from socially conservative to radical. In some parts of the country, NOW members protested in the streets, in corporation headquarters, and in churches; in other places, NOW members preferred quieter campaigns of persuasion. This jumble of activism styles gave both conservatives and progressives something to dislike about the young group, even within NOW's own membership.

At the second annual conference, tension between conservative and radical members bubbled to the surface, carrying important consequences for the organization. Conference business called for establishing NOW's Bill of Rights, requiring attendees to decide on NOW's policy for several controversial issues. The ERA was the first issue to crack the organization. Many of the early leaders of NOW were active in the labor movement and represented unions that had fought hard for legislation protecting female workers; the ERA would spell the end of these policies. But protective legislation had proved to be an effective tool in keeping women out of better-paying industries and jobs. Outside of the labor contingent, most NOW members considered the ERA to be a necessary part of achieving equality. When the motion passed to include the ERA as a part of NOW's platform, the union women resigned their positions, exiting the organization. It is worth noting, though, that many of these women, while loyal to the labor movement, also continued to put pressure on their unions to change their official positions on protective legislation. Within a year, for example, Carolyn Davis, the former secretary for national NOW, had convinced the United Auto Workers to endorse the ERA (Davis 1999).

The next issue to drive a wedge in the young organization was abortion (see chapter 3 for an extended discussion of this schism). Abortion was only just emerging as a topic of public debate, and many feminists remained uncomfortable with the issue. This was particularly true of older, midwestern members, who wanted to focus instead on inequality, education, and employment. Younger, East Coast members pressed the issue, successfully insisting that the repeal of abortion restrictions was a critical component in establishing women's freedom to live the lives they wanted. When the abortion plank passed, a group of members from the Midwest walked out, including Elizabeth "Betty" Boyer, a member of the national board of directors.

These early schisms are the first of many examples of the broad diversity NOW encompassed. Even in these earliest years, NOW's challenge was to build a stable and sustainable national organization while cultivating and capitalizing on the sense of urgency coming from its grassroots membership (Barakso 2004). Some leaders were better at one side of this job than the other. Betty Friedan (2000, 185) wrote of her aggravation at any time spent on structure or "internal housekeeping," believing this to be time stolen from activism. She came to loathe NOW's meetings devoted to routine organizational maintenance:

> I began to get headaches and to start impatiently tapping my foot
> under the tables when our finicky lawyers felt it necessary to change
> the by-laws yet again, or to describe the endless red tape we still had
> to negotiate to get tax-exempt status for our legal defense fund. . . .
> I just wanted to get out there and *do* it.

Even in NOW, the organization held as the epitome of formalized bureaucracy in the feminist movement, leaders divided on how bureaucratic they should be and on how much time needed to be spent on maintaining the organization. But structural issues proved to be critical over the first years of the organization, with members at the local level growing increasingly frustrated at the lack of routinized access to national NOW and its unresponsiveness to their needs.

Indeed, NOW did experience a steep learning curve in its early years as leaders and members wrangled over authority and structure. For various reasons, including an onslaught of demand from women all over the country that created runaway momentum, founders neglected to create clear and binding ties between the local and national levels. As a result, NOW's early years were plagued with fights—even lawsuits—over the best balance of power between local and national interests. These fights included protracted battles over how federated levels should be incorporated and how resources should be properly balanced and shared across the organization.

It took time for NOW's younger members—some of whom were new to feminism and some of whom came to NOW after spending time in small collectives—to adjust to formalized organizational life. Those with deeper organizational résumés, such as those who had participated with the League of Women Voters, helped craft NOW's structure and tone over its first years so that it increasingly matched the bureaucratic wrangling common in other political organizations. In her interview for the Tully–Crenshaw Feminist Oral History Project, Mary Jean Tully (1992) remembered a spirited 1974 annual conference in Houston when different factions of leaders campaigned against each other for the first time:

> I remember standing in the back strategizing . . . saying, "We've got to get this microphone covered, and we've got to do this, we've got to do that," and loving it, because that's the way we'd done things in the League of Women Voters, much more dispassionately, over issues than over people. But they were great political strategists in the LWV, and you didn't go into a convention without having—if you were trying to get your agenda adopted, you didn't go in without having everybody lined up, and knowing how you were going to fight. . . . The NOW people, at least in the beginning . . . didn't know too much about such things.

In her explanation, Tully notes that many NOW members lacked prior experience in traditional political organizations and were uncomfortable with the politics that came with contentious conventions and elections. In contrast, many of NOW's national leaders called on their prior experience in "dispassionate" political organizations. They channeled their conflicts through routine elections and agenda setting. Over time, NOW members and leaders grew more experienced, acclimating to the norms of a formalized political organization, and, as the story goes, internal factionalism became less common.

Leaders and members further elaborated the bureaucratic structure, creating more space for cultures and styles that were locally meaningful. At the same time, the national structure grew more formalized, adding layers of state and regional representation that tied the local level more closely to national identity and policy. The additional organizational layers also enhanced opportunities for local members to work their way up the organizational ladder into national leadership. In this common version of NOW's story, the organization found resolutions for its early conflicts in greater formalization and elaboration of the bureaucracy, with centralized leadership at the top and broad freedom at the local level. Operating together, these organizational elements kept the organization from disastrous factionalism and schism.

In its current form, NOW is governed by a small group of elected executive officers, a large board of directors, and roughly thirty paid staff (Barakso 2004), who make up the national level of the organization. NOW's national officers are elected by the delegates from chapters at the annual conferences. Beneath the national level, NOW is organized into nine regions, fifty state chapters, and more than six hundred local chapters. Its federated structure allows NOW to have a foot in the politics at each level of government. At the same time, grassroots members have autonomy to pursue whichever parts of the broad national agenda resonate with them, or even to choose separate projects so long as they do not conflict with the national agenda. The loose, organizational arrangement between national and local levels has been lauded by social movement scholars for allowing national organizations to attract and maintain members with diverse interests and skills, while aggregating resources toward a common national agenda (McCarthy 2005).

In addition to its federated structure, NOW also expanded horizontally to include a variety of organizational divisions. In the earliest period of NOW, leaders created dozens of task forces and committees, each focusing on a particular issue or tactic. As I discuss in chapter 5, over the years, the number of issues NOW includes has expanded and contracted. There is constant pressure from members to expand NOW's domain to new issues. At its high point, national NOW included more than thirty distinct task forces. But there are real limitations to how many different areas an organization, even one as large as NOW, can effectively manage. By 2017, NOW's national priorities had evolved to include just five main issues—the "sex-abuse-to-prison pipeline," the ERA, reproductive justice, voting rights, and immigrant rights. Beyond these core priorities, however, NOW continues to maintain a variety of working groups and committees devoted to other issues.

While leaders and members struggled over the right balance of issues on which to focus internally, NOW expanded by creating satellite organizations—legally distinct organizations that share NOW's brand identity but exist under different tax designations. When people refer to NOW, they most commonly mean the membership organization. NOW branched beyond this single form in 1971 to form a nonprofit legal and education fund, followed quickly by a system of political action committees operating at the federal and state levels and the NOW Foundation. These organizations represent an expansion of NOW's bureaucracy, although they vary in how closely they overlap with NOW, the membership organization.

Ironically, given the often pessimistic view of how grassroots members fare in bureaucracies, NOW added to and elaborated its structure precisely to increase the influence of member voices at the local levels of the organization. It was a compromise to maximize the autonomy of members and enhance the ties between leaders and members while providing direction and unity for a large and geographically dispersed organization. NOW's expansive bureaucratic structure and agenda create space for members to pursue the kind of feminism they want in whatever way they want. This underscores the paradox of NOW's remarkable inclusiveness, stability, and longevity, even as it split, again and again. The central focus of this book is to understand how this structure has not only failed to inhibit factionalism and splitting but also facilitated organizational splitting. The following chapters are devoted to understanding each of these structural elements and detailing how internal conflict grew because of them.

Data Sources

I collected data for this study over a period of seven years from a variety of sources, including original interviews, archives, and secondary histories of the cases (see the appendix). I located cases of factionalism and schisms in NOW through a secondary literature search that included academic, biographical, and historical accounts of the American feminist movement. As noted, low-level conflict is often ubiquitous in social movement organizations, making it difficult to delineate the differences between run-of-the-mill membership grousing, infighting, and full-blown factionalism. In choosing cases to include, I rely on how the activists themselves describe the events. I also included groups whom other NOW members or historians have characterized as having broken away from NOW.

Inevitably, there is some slippage in trying to define this phenomenon. I do not claim to have found all of the episodes of factionalism and breaking away that occurred across NOW's fifty-year history. Because of the general challenges in tracking small, new, and local groups (Blee 2012), the factionalism most likely to be underrepresented here is at the local level. Generally, there is more and better data available for organizations operating at the national level. Nevertheless, the cases I do discuss in these pages represent a wide swath of activism across time, geography, and organizational location.

To understand how these cases of factionalism developed, I drew from multiple sets of oral histories and interviews, including the Tully–Crenshaw Feminist Oral History Project (Schlesinger Library 2007), the Voices of Feminism Oral History Project (Sophia Smith Collection 2006), the Washington Women's History Consortium (Lonnquist 2007), and original interviews I conducted in 2009 and 2010. The interviewees were overwhelmingly white and from middle-class backgrounds and ranged in age from their mid-thirties to their late eighties at the time of the interviews. Most of them were active in the early years of NOW and they varied in how long they stayed active in the organization from just a few years to several decades. All interviewees agreed to be identified by their real names. I chose interviewees for their knowledge of how these episodes of factionalism unfolded or for their participation in the breakaway organizations after a schism occurred. Where possible, I triangulated data between the interviews, archival sources, and histories of the movement to confirm accounts. Where there are discrepancies between accounts, I present all perspectives of what occurred.

I also collected archival data from the Schlesinger Library at Harvard University, which houses NOW's organizational documents, as well as the papers of individual leaders and members who have elected to donate their materials. I chose documents based on the libraries' subject guides, which indicated where there was material relevant to the factions. These documents included correspondence sent from factions to NOW members, members' letters and reports to the board, and personal correspondence between leaders. For several groups, I was also able to locate newsletters and publications that detailed their origins and continuing relationships with other organizations, including NOW.

NOW's own website also contains a treasure trove of data covering its organizational history and timelines. Most useful, for the purposes of this book, were two sets of documents—NOW's issue manuals, specifying the official positions NOW has adopted over time, and its administrative policy manuals, covering NOW's administrative and structural changes over time. Both detail the evolution of the organization from June 1966 to October 2014, providing a kind of road map for how NOW has responded over time to its internal battles and external pressures. The combination of organizational documents and members' own accounts of factionalism has proved to be invaluable in piecing together how the fights unfolded and how they shaped NOW over time.

Plan of the Book

In chapter 2, I elaborate on the theoretical orientation introduced here. I detail the way the social movements and organizational scholars have understood the role of formalized bureaucratic organizations. While acknowledging stability and longevity, I lay out my argument for how these forms also contribute to organizational factionalism and splitting by creating pockets for multiple collective identities to flourish in a single structure.

In chapter 3, I examine how NOW's federated structure created space for local NOW members to differentiate their chapters from the national organization. By shifting to more closely match their local contexts, grassroots chapters drifted from NOW leaders in substantial and sometimes irreparable ways. When factions emerged, local members often grew frustrated at their inability to expand their localized identities, strategies, and priorities to the rest of the organization. Their isolation often means local factions without the resources they need to effectively express their voices, leaving them with only the options of staying members in a poorly fitting organization or leaving NOW to create a new group from scratch.

In chapter 4, I clarify the structural relationships introduced in chapter 2 by comparing local factions to those that emerged at NOW's national level. This comparison reveals that not all factions are created equal; some are born in circumstances that make breaking away less appealing, less possible, and less necessary. Factionalism has occurred in every part of NOW's structure, but those factions that develop within the board of directors have special resources to use in their fights and an increased commitment to NOW's success. Factions emerging at NOW's national level illuminate constraints on grassroots factions, which struggle to gain traction outside of their own local areas and have few options for continuing their fight inside of NOW.

In chapter 5, I shift my attention to the organizational splits that emerged from NOW's task forces and committees. Designed to efficiently manage its broad agenda, NOW's task forces effectively created pathways for members to innovate and incubate niche collective identities. At the same time, these task forces were chronically underserved by NOW's administrative structure. The combination of these factors made breaking away seem both feasible and attractive for many groups. I close chapter 5 with a brief discussion of how and why this pattern may have shifted in NOW over time.

Chapter 6 offers a view into how NOW expanded its organizational reach by creating a system of satellite organizations. Large, bureaucratic groups like NOW are well positioned to raise money from tax-exempt donations by intentionally breaking off some functions into new, freestanding organizations. But splitting in this way also creates significant organizational dilemmas, as leaders in both groups struggle jointly to define their relationships and to balance their diverging interests. In these cases, environmental pressures drive the initial splits, but NOW and organizations like it face continuing consequences of this kind of pragmatic schism.

In the Conclusion, I review the bureaucratic model of splitting before closing with a discussion of why schisms are not always a bad thing. I pick up the argument, begun here, that splitting apart can have significant benefits for the group that breaks away, for the original organization, and for the broader movement they continue to inhabit. While these splits are often painful, they can also generate new and important spaces expanding the social movement, allowing more people outlets for participation. In this moment of deep political uncertainty and revitalized feminist mobilization, organizational splits are likely to become more common. As the evidence presented throughout this book demonstrates, this is also a positive sign for the future of feminism.

CHAPTER TWO

Bureaucracies, Boundaries, and Splitting

Conflict within social movement organizations is inevitable. At some point, members will disagree with each other over any number of issues, including how to structure their organization, what tactics they should use, what goals they should pursue, what ideology should unite them, and how they should divide up their (usually meager) resources. Conflict, in other words, is ubiquitous, and there is no shortage of reasons for members to fight with each other. In his foundational work on the successes and failures of movement organizations, William A. Gamson (1990) calls factionalism a misery few groups avoid.

Factionalism has received a good deal of attention from scholars, and the social movements literature is divided between efforts to explain how conflict affects movements and explorations of the organizational characteristics that correlate with factionalism. In the first strain of literature, scholars have mostly found the misery to which Gamson refers. When conflict among members erupts, scholars have traditionally argued that it initiates a brutal cycle of organizational decline. Factions coalesce and compete for power, denigrating each other as a way to attract members to their respective sides; as the factions grow further apart, the conflict consumes ever greater amounts of organizational energy, time, and money to manage it (Frey, Dietz, and Kalof 1992). When leaders fail to contain the conflict, their group splits apart or dissolves completely, tarnished with the label of organizational failure. In this tradition, factionalism is the worst fate that can befall an organization. Douglas McAdam (1982), for example, argues that the civil rights movement was weakened by infighting among and within its groups, reducing its political influence at critical moments. A small but growing group of scholars have bucked this fatalism, arguing that some internal conflict can help groups clarify priorities, solidify members' commitments, and mobilize new, creative activism (Benford 1993; Ferree and Hess 2002; Ghaziani 2008; Luna 2010; McCammon 2015).

If movement scholars found little agreement about whether factionalism was good or bad, they found common ground in predicting which organizations were most prone to the outcome. All groups might experience conflict, but some kinds of groups should be better able to channel it in ways that reaffirm group commitment. This literature relies on the assumption that formalized structures are the key to reducing and routing conflict. Formalization refers to a group of mutually reinforcing characteristics, including bureaucratic structures; centralized decision-making; professionalized leaders and staff; written rules and procedures; and a division of labor, often in a federated form. Although no group can escape internal strife completely, written procedures, bylaws, and regular elections tame members' disagreements by steering them through routine, predictable competitions.

Formalized bureaucracies are supposed to be good at managing conflict for a number of related reasons. First, the kinds of groups that adopt these forms may already have some immunity to dramatic schisms. They tend to be broadly inclusive, requiring very little of members beyond occasional dues paying. Their loose criteria for membership and relaxed "doctrinal orthodoxy" (Zald and Ash 1966, 337) mean that inclusive bureaucracies can recruit members with wide-ranging ideas about tactics, strategies, and goals as well as members who are willing to tolerate this kind of diversity. There are groups like this in every social movement; the best-known examples are the Sierra Club in the environmental movement, the NAACP in the civil rights movement, and NOW in the feminist movement. Writing about NOW's stability as a broadly inclusive organization, Alice Echols (1989, 200) states that it had been "nowhere nearly as fractious as most radical feminist groups, and it was considerably more accepting of women who did not yet know that in some feminist circles high heels and make-up were evidence of collaboration." All could join and find a place somewhere in the sprawling organization.

A second feature of bureaucratic groups that scholars have argued minimize factionalism is their complex and segmented structures (Balser 1997; King 2008). Bureaucracies develop elaborate internal boundaries that corral members into different locations, arranged both vertically into hierarchies and horizontally into distinct committees, task forces, and satellite groups. Federated structures are useful in that they allow organizations to extend from a national level down to a wide base of local communities, providing a blueprint for starting new chapters and establishing local leadership. Grassroots affiliates are free to manage their own affairs and create locally meaningful styles of activism, even within a national organization. Local chapters develop specific collective identities, which can be quite different from chapters in other geographical locations. NOW offers an excellent example of this kind of segmentation (Lofland 1996; Mueller 1995; Freeman 1975). Beginning with just two levels—a national and a local—NOW eventually developed a fully federated structure with clusters of local chapters, state chapters, and regional divisions. Scholars have argued that this arrangement reduced conflict by letting local chapters carve out their own internal mini-organizations that function more or less autonomously (Reger 2002a, 2002b; Reger and Staggenborg 2006).

Similarly, horizontal expansion allows organizations to establish a broad "niche width," taking on multiple—sometimes dozens—of issues and projects and dividing the work among committees, task forces, and satellite groups (Carroll 1985). Sometimes called "full service public interest organization[s]" (Shaiko 1999; see also Andrews et al. 2010), organizational ecologists have argued that this approach allows groups to "compete in a variety of domains simultaneously" (Carroll 1985, 1266). For organizational ecologists and many social movement theorists, this orientation makes strategic sense—a generalist orientation is a hedge against both too much success and not enough on any single issue. If a single-issue group achieves its goal, it faces a crisis about what to do next. Its raison d'être has evaporated, and unless it can find something new on which to focus, supporters consider the organization no longer necessary. In the case of too little success, a single-issue organization faces a long haul in keeping members and supporters interested in what must seem an increasingly hopeless cause. A generalist orientation helps weather both successes and failures, allowing for seamless shifts in group priorities. Bureaucratic groups can divide their large membership among many simultaneous issues, insulating themselves from declining resources in any one area. Theoretically, members in these groups need not fight over priorities because they can focus on any issue they want.

Third, and related, a segmented and federated structure allows bureaucratic groups to recruit and compartmentalize a diverse range of activists to cover their broad agenda. Bureaucratic groups become dense networks of task forces, committees, satellite organizations, and action centers. Each smaller membership cluster has a limited scope, working on a single issue of the broader agenda. This narrowing can be a healthy compromise in organizations like NOW, where a generalist orientation—taking on dozens of issues at any given time—can be overwhelming to individual members and chapters. By focusing on a smaller set of issues, chapters can create a localized collective identity tailored to what its members care most about. Similarly, members who volunteer for specific issue committees create their own subculture of specialized knowledge and values. They join a committee because they already care deeply about its particular focus, and their subsequent committee work reinforces their passion. In organizations with tens of thousands of members, these smaller subgroups help individuals establish more intimate connections and a sense of community. This arrangement also makes it easier to recruit ever more members by providing a blueprint for expanding to new issues and new geographical areas. In theory, this works to prevent factionalism because each membership cluster can do its work in whatever way makes the most sense for its specific context, without needing constantly to negotiate with other members holding different values.

This division of labor often means that bureaucratic groups hire specialized staff and leaders to focus on skilled activism, such as legal advocacy and political lobbying. Because of the state's regulatory policies for raising tax-exempt money, bureaucratic movement groups often spin out these specialists into separate, satellite organizations. The U.S. government generally requires activist groups to separate their political advocacy work from their charitable or educational work. To maximize their strategic reach, formalized bureaucracies engage in all of these tasks simultaneously by creating systems of organizations, separated only by flimsy and perforated boundaries. As with a federated structure, this division of labor is supposed to minimize conflict because members can focus on (or neglect) any issues they want and are free to engage in political advocacy without jeopardizing the tax-exempt status of the satellite groups. The structure also creates greater organizational stability because the group maximizes its resources, while subgroups focus on specific priorities, all while maintaining a single organizational brand. All of these features should work together to limit factionalism. By bounding members off into distinct internally homogenous clusters, bureaucratic groups reduce points of friction between members.

Despite the myriad benefits of this form, bureaucratic organizations are also thought to pay a heavy price. At worst, critics fear that bureaucratic leaders may hoard decision-making, alienating members from any real attachment to their group (Chen, Lune, and Queen 2013). At best, if we accept that the bureaucratic form reduces factionalism, scholars argue that this robs groups of the conflict needed to spur innovative movement theories, strategies, and identities (Mueller 1995). Bureaucratic forms, critics argue, squeeze out painful but productive conflict, in pursuit of stability, legitimacy, and resources (Fitzgerald and Rodgers 2000; Piven and Cloward 1977).

In this line of thought, flat organizational structures lead to greater creativity because members must fight their way toward a group consensus. Informal collectives are bursting with creative energy precisely because they lack stabilizing structures that reduce internal conflict. They reject boundaries that mark different kinds of work or official roles among members and rotate responsibilities as insurance against inequality. They eschew elaborated levels, elected offices, division of labor, and written procedures, relying instead on principles of consensus and close personal relationships to make decisions. On top of the philosophical mandate that hierarchy should be avoided, these organizational preferences are supposed to unleash an avalanche of creativity. All voices are heard and proposed solutions must find a consensus to move forward. Under these conditions, members will produce new ways of thinking that press the movement in new directions.

This framing of organizational structures often takes on a moral tone. As Francesca Polletta (2005) argues, organizational choices are never simply instrumental because activists filter these decisions through their particular cultural and symbolic associations. Collectivist structures are regularly proffered as the higher moral choice—a rejection of the conservative and masculine organizational forms used to oppress powerless people throughout society. Kathleen J. Fitzgerald and Diane M. Rodgers (2000), in defining radical social movement organizations, embrace this frame, arguing that bureaucratic groups are reformist in nature, seeking resources and organizational stability at the expense of a truly free and radical agenda.

Many of the young organizers in the latest surge of American activism have favored flat organizational structures. Echoing what many scholars have written about the benefits of a collectivist structure, ShiShi Rose, who operated the social media accounts for the Women's March, claimed their organizing approach had "given people involved in it a new outlook on what female leadership is supposed to look like" (Cusumano 2017). In the same interview, other Women's March organizers asserted that their "diffuse, decentralized structure will ensure [participants] aren't answering to one leader," with the hope that the "movement will outlast any particular demonstration."

Leaders in other contemporary movements have eschewed building bureaucratic infrastructure as well. Following several high-profile deaths of African Americans at the hands of police officers, the Black Lives Matter movement mobilized as a loose network of groups and chapters across the country. Black Lives Matter activists have "intentionally departed[ed]" from the "centralized patriarchal leadership that scuttled other black-led political organizations" (Sands 2017). In practice, this means that founders rejected forming a national administration that could coordinate actions across the country. Instead, new chapters are reviewed by the network of existing chapters. Leadership is "diffused among autonomous chapters," in a structure "design[ed]" to mystify outsiders (Touré 2017). According to academic Peniel Joseph (2017), the lack of national coordination is a benefit: "we actually have people doing work and organizing, and it's not a top down hierarchical leadership structure."

Occupy Wall Street famously rejected formalizing its structure after emerging in fall 2011, first in New York City and soon after in communities across the nation. Occupy began as a protest against increasing economic inequality and unchecked power of corporate money in politics. It quickly branched to include a variety of institutional targets beyond Wall Street. Occupy's organizing principle was shared power, expressed through flat group structures, volunteerism, and members' equal time at meetings. Early in its mobilization, proponents delighted in its diffused leadership and creative forms. They made many of the same arguments organizers in Black Lives Matter and the Women's March have—a lack of hierarchy, they claimed, would make it a better community, more inclusive, and more creative, because the organizing work was spread among all participants.

If these activists were deeply optimistic about the benefits of informal flat structures, they also experienced the weaknesses of this form for managing conflict. Without formalized structures and standardized rules, flat organizations have few administrative methods for channeling the energy of internal dissent. Occupy never developed into a cohesive movement. Within a year, its activists were splitting over how and whether to maintain consensus decision-making processes as well who could claim the Occupy label (Cuddy 2011; McVeigh 2011). Local Black Lives Matter groups have also struggled with the challenges of a "structureless" movement and have begun demanding greater accountability from de facto national leaders, access to funding and resources, and a unifying vision and strategy that could bring the local groups together (Sands 2017). And while the national leaders of Women's March shifted their momentum to electoral politics with a voter registration and mobilization campaign for the 2018 mid-term elections (Women's March 2017), local affiliates are struggling to define the boundaries and missions of their groups. In some places, paralyzing fights have emerged over issues of racial identity politics with no clear path for resolving the problems other than dissolving the group altogether. In Portland, Oregon, just over a year after forming, Women's March moderators announced their intention to shutter the group's main Facebook page, which has served as its primary organizing forum (Women's March on Portland 2017), and to create a second, more exclusive page.

These are not new struggles. In the 1970s, antinuclear group Clamshell Alliance formulated their structure as a conscious rejection of the "hierarchical excesses" of the New Left movement (Mitchell 1981, 82). The group was enormously successful in attracting media attention to its direct-action tactics, but its attempts to establish a national consensus process slowed group decision-making to a crawl. When quick decisions were required, members of the national coordinating committee were forced to break with the consensus process, sowing discord among those who felt disenfranchised. Members also disagreed about what kinds of actions were most likely to stop the construction of new plants. Unable to find consensus or an acceptable compromise, and with no other structures in place to make decisions, the group split into two distinct organizations. The schism took a toll on the resulting groups, and by 1981, both had dissolved (Downey 1986). Similarly, 1970s women's liberation collectives collapsed at the peak of their movement's mobilization, when their informal structures were unable to accommodate the influx of new members. Members bitterly divided over how to manage their increasing differences, ultimately breaking off into tiny splinter groups or dropping out completely (Mueller 1995; Polletta 2002).

The organizational dilemma seems intractable—flat, informal structures facilitate greater creativity and freedom but seem doomed to debilitating factionalism unless they stay small and homogenous. Bureaucracies, so stable and predictable, are able to grow large and diverse by channeling and suppressing conflict among members. Yet conflict provides the engine for greater creativity and transformative ideology. Bureaucracies might experience some low-level conflict, but their elaborate infrastructure tames it in ways that limit both member creativity and factionalism.

This book presents evidence that we should rethink this problem. First, although bureaucratic organizations may be more stable, they are often filled with the same kinds of generative conflicts that play out in small collectives. As we will see, many of the same activists fighting in small feminist collectives were also members of NOW, and they pressed for their progressive organizational ideals there too. Elaborate, hierarchical structures did not squash these conflicts, nor did they always route those conflicts in the predicted ways.

Second, while bureaucratic movement groups enjoy greater stability by quickly escaping the traps of newness and smallness (Edwards and Marullo 1995; Hannan and Freeman 1988; Minkoff 1995), they are not split-proof. Rather, because bureaucratic structures provide a high degree of stability, we tend to overlook or minimize the schisms they do experience. In fact, across the social movements literature, there is plenty of evidence of bureaucratic splitting, yet we have failed to incorporate these cases into our organizational theory because they often do not look like the schisms we expect. We tend to restrict our examinations of factionalism and schism to those that break a parent organization in half, paralyzing or killing the entire group, rather than understanding how extended conflict plays out in large, hierarchic structures (King 2008). The large size and broad scope of bureaucratic groups mean that members can regularly break away to start new independent organizations without seriously threatening the parent's survival. Bureaucratic parent groups can remain alive and stable through a surprisingly high number of splits, and their survival makes us less likely to recognize the organizational splitting they do experience.

We also tend to overemphasize combative schisms, when members are particularly vituperative in their battles with each other. Yet many organizational splits occur without caustic battles. Members can decide they have no future within the parent group, while choosing to maintain a working relationship after splitting away. The literature is more likely to frame these kinds of splits as organizational spin-offs, lacking the kind of generative conflict present in smaller collectives. I argue that even when they appear to be simple bureaucratic spin-offs, these splits are often rooted in deeper, more interesting, and more generative conflict than we typically credit them.

Finally, and most importantly, the bureaucratic structures that provide such stability and longevity to movement groups also *create* distinct kinds of factionalization and splitting. Because of their size, scope, and shape, movement bureaucracies are a trove of particular kinds of conflict to which we have paid remarkably little attention. By shining a light on bureaucratic splits, we can begin to reconcile their nature as both stable workhorses and creative engines in the social movements they inhabit.

A Theory of Bureaucratic Splitting

As I discussed earlier, formalized and bureaucratic movement groups are defined, in part, by their larger membership, broad agendas, and segmented structures. Each of these features helps make the overall organization stable, even as it also produces conditions for membership splits. While critics fear that formalized bureaucracy inescapably leads to centralized decision-making, a variety of research finds the opposite. Formalized bureaucracies are frequently decentralized, generalist organizations comprising diverse groups mobilized around a broader range of resources. This arrangement provides a great deal of autonomy for subunits to carry out their work in the ways that make sense in their specific and local contexts (see Scott 2003 for a review of this literature). Within their smaller clusters, members enjoy relative autonomy and freedom to do their work in the ways that make the most sense to them. Rather than a dictate coming from the top of the organization, they independently decide what projects, targets, and collective identities make the best fit for their subgroup. To borrow from organizational ecology again, we can see that even within an overall generalist structure, specialist subgroups develop and thrive in peripheral organizational locations (Carroll 1985). While this structure has clear benefits of mobilizing a wide range of people and resources, it is also vulnerable to alienation and conflict among some subgroups. This risk becomes clearer when we examine the ways bureaucracies are divided into core and peripheral areas.

Bureaucratic Core and Periphery

In the language of open systems organizational theory, membership subgroups are not created equally within bureaucracies but are instead arranged along a continuum moving from the "core" of an organization to its "periphery" (Scott 2003).

In movement organizations, the core generally includes national leaders or boards of directors, executive positions, and administrative committees. The periphery includes those groups with less structural power, including local and state chapters as well as satellite organizations. The organization's agenda is also divided into core priorities, which receive greater attention and resources from core leaders, and peripheral priorities, which receive less consideration. Particular issues might shift back and forth between the core and periphery over time, becoming centrally important to an organization in specific historical moments, only to fade back to the periphery as the cultural or political context changes. These

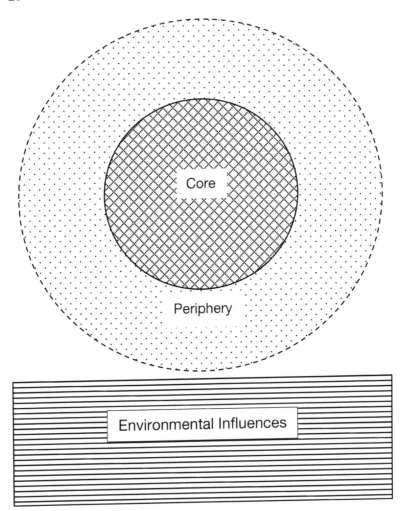

Bureaucratic core and periphery.

distinct organizational relationships set into motion a variety of mechanisms for membership splits. Being located in the core versus the periphery affects members' freedom to differentiate from the rest of the organization, access to organizational power and resources, and their relationships with external communities. I deal with each of these mechanisms in turn, as well as with several moderating factors.

From the open systems perspective, bureaucratic freedom and power

Origin of faction	Core	Periphery
Example locations	National board of directors Executive committees Prioritized task forces	Local chapters Nonprioritized task forces Satellite organizations
Accessible resources	Money Power	Freedom External relationships
Outcome	Less likely to break away	More likely to break away
Moderating conditions	Expanding/declining movement Time period–issue connection Developed infrastructure	

Mechanisms for bureaucratic splitting.

operate as two sides of the same coin. Despite its negative connotations, bureaucratization creates pockets of freedom in which members can pursue new and creative identities, ideologies, and tactics. But this freedom is not evenly distributed across the organization. The national level of the organization codifies policies and sets priorities; it represents the overall organizational brand and balances the interests of geographically and culturally diverse members. These responsibilities often mean that the bureaucratic core will strike moderate, balanced positions designed to satisfy the highest possible number of members and external supporters. Membership clusters operating in the national core are more tightly hemmed in by these responsibilities, giving them less room to experiment with their organizational identity. In outer locations, membership clusters are isolated from the administrative oversight of national leaders. In fact, bureaucratic administrators can formally and informally encourage peripheral diversity and variation to better recruit members. Some peripheral clusters remain closely aligned with the core; others will grow in radical or conservative directions. Whatever their orientation, peripheral clusters will reflect the values and sensibilities of their local contexts. Operating on the organizational margins means these clusters will be freer to develop idiosyncratic collective identities at odds with the national core.

NOW offers instructive examples of this arrangement. Its subunits, such as its local chapters, issue committees, and tax-exempt satellite organizations, have traditionally had significant latitude to make independent decisions in setting priorities and organizing their internal power relationships. While the national level of NOW had a set of bylaws mandating particular forms, Jo Freeman (1975, 230) noted that "many new chapters just disregarded the national-proposed structure and created their own. The Berkeley chapter . . . ha[d] three conveners, which divide[d] up among themselves the usual duties of chapter officers." Similarly, NOW's task forces and Legal Defense and Education Fund (NOW LDEF) were free to determine their own priorities and styles of activism in accordance with their particular goals and external audiences. In this way, its decentralized bureaucratic structure allowed multiple collective identities to flourish under a single organizational umbrella. This pattern is also evident in other large, formalized movement organizations. Leslie King (2008, 59n18), in her study of ideological conflict in the Sierra Club, found that its decentralized democratic structure created ideological gaps between factionalized membership groups and the professional staff at the core of the organization. Peripheral member groups were able to stay and fight for their preferences precisely because the decentralized democratic structure continued to give them space. However, structural freedom opens the possibility that some membership clusters will grow in ways fundamentally at odds with the core of the organization, causing them to weigh the benefits of formally breaking away.

Of course, factionalism can also develop at the core of an organization, with leaders clashing over the direction of the organization. However, national leadership factions are less likely to have developed serious ideological inconsistencies with the broader organization. After all, the organization's written rules and procedures are shaped by these very self-selected members. They also have more organizational tools and resources at their disposal. Unlike factions operating in peripheral locations, core subgroups have routine access to decision-making and access to other influential national leaders. They are better able to reach members across the geographical spread of the organization, and their prominence as national leaders gives them special legitimacy in persuading rank-and-file members of their positions. Finally, they are better able to use and manipulate the decentralized bureaucratic structure to their advantage than are groups operating from marginal locations. These factors jointly operate to keep core factions from breaking away.

The wider the gap between a peripheral group's collective identity and the national organization's core, the more pressure there will be to exit. Albert O. Hirschman (1970) famously argues that, when members are unhappy with their group, their decision to stay or to leave is conditioned on the amount of loyalty they feel toward their group. Members with the greatest loyalty stay and protest the things they do not like, as opposed to exiting at the first sign of trouble. But member loyalty is complicated in large, decentralized movement organizations. Peripheral members develop distinct collective identities, giving them locally rooted definitions of who counts as "us" and who counts as "them," the antagonists against which the group defines itself (Hunt, Benford, and Snow 1994; Reger 2008). It is easy to see how more specific loyalty ties develop. In many peripheral locations, members are attached to each other not just through organizational duties and abstract commitments; they also share a common community and personal history with each other. They work with each other frequently; they go to school together; they know each other's families. These bonds exist in the context of the parent organization, but they also exist outside of and apart from it. In creating smaller membership clusters, bureaucratic groups raise the possibility that members will develop a localized "us" that diverges substantially from the rest of the organization. In this case, leaders and comembers may become the "thems-inside" whom factional members work against (Gamson 1997). This gives peripheral factions more confidence that they could persist as fully independent groups without the larger organization as well as the ability to break away without violating their deeper loyalties.

Pressure to break away comes from the mismatch between *freedom* and *power*. While peripheral clusters have a great deal of freedom, they have little structural power. Insulation from administrative oversight also means they are isolated from levers of power that might help them get what they want. In large bureaucratic organizations, routine decision-making happens in the core, by the board of directors or executive committees. Peripheral clusters do not have routine access to this process.

Instead, they have only indirect input—by voting for representatives or making bylaw proposals—but these are ineffective ways to realign the broader organization with a peripheral group's preferences. Under these circumstances, peripheral groups, having drifted far from the core and having few organizational tools available, are likely to see breaking away as the preferable option.

Internal pressure to break away or to stay is also shaped by members' relationships to the *external environment*. A defining insight of both the open systems and political opportunity perspectives is that what happens inside of organizations is deeply connected to and shaped by what is happening outside of them (Davis et al. 2005; Zald, Morrill, and Rao 2005; Balser 1997; McAdam 1982; Meyer 2004; Scott 2003; Weber and Waeger 2017). But not all parts of the organization are equally susceptible to the influences from the environment. More than clusters at the core of the organization, peripheral clusters are shaped by forces outside the organization. At the organizational edges, members have idiosyncratic experiences and community connections, sometimes leading them to distinct conclusions about the best tactics, strategies, and ideologies. To borrow language from Scott (2003), peripheral clusters are more vulnerable to environmental winds, and their ideologies, identities, and priorities can be shifted in ways that diverge from their parent organizations.

This can happen in multiple ways. To recruit new members or form partnerships, peripheral clusters need to achieve at least some minimal amount of local legitimacy by conforming to contemporary and specific norms in their community (Scott 2003). Through local recruiting and partnerships, peripheral clusters build bridges from their group to the outside world. These bridges carry the group's ideas out into the world, but they are also conduits by which the world's ideas enter the group. Over these bridges, new perspectives can enter and shift how the local chapter thinks about its national organization. Large, bureaucratic organizations are vulnerable to this problem because their prominent national reputation can be a poor fit for local activist communities. In some cases, the national organization is perceived as too conservative for the more radically oriented local community. The same organization may be perceived as too radical in conservative communities. In either case, peripheral members often struggle to balance the reputation of their national organization with the local environment in which they carry out their work.

Similarly, members working on a peripheralized task force in their organization will likely seek to work with external activists and groups in their issue domain. If these external partners have negative attitudes toward the parent group, peripheral committees might begin to weigh the relative benefits of staying or breaking away. By definition, peripheral issues receive meager resources and attention; under these conditions, task force members might decide that the costs of association with the parent are too high and the benefits too low to warrant staying. This is the price of embracing a decentralized and hierarchical structure. Isolation of peripheral locations reinforces any growing collective-identity differences, while strengthening peripheral clusters' relationships with external groups.

For satellite groups, the tax-exempt sister organizations to the membership group, tensions with core leaders can be particularly severe. Satellite groups need to maintain legitimacy from fairly conservative outside actors like state regulators and funders. Even as satellite organizations are cultivating quieter and more reserved reputations, members of the parent organization may continue to use direct-action or other "expressive" tactics that can be off-putting to elites outside the movement. While they share a brand and organizational umbrella with a membership organization, they have no control over what the membership side is doing. When satellite groups are too much lumped together with a more boisterous membership organization, they jeopardize important environmental relationships and critical resources. Under this tension, peripheral groups will try to put greater distance between themselves and the parent organization, even to the point of severing their ties completely.

Moderating Factors

In comparison to core factions, peripheral factions will face greater pushes out of the parent organization and fewer loyalty pulls to stay inside. Some conditions moderate this basic relationship, including an expanding or contracting social movement, increasing or decreasing issue salience, and the amount of developed organizational infrastructure. I deal with each in the following pages.

Expanding and Contracting Social Movement

Resource mobilization, political opportunity, and organizational theorists have long pointed to the ways environmental conditions shape the founding rates and mortality of organizations (Jenkins 1983; McCarthy and Zald 1977; Meyer 2004; Singh and Lumsden 1990). The same conditions that lead the founding of new organizations likely affect factions' decisions about breaking away. During periods of economic growth and movement expansion, organizational factions, no matter where they originate, have greater incentives to break away. Factions have a better chance of surviving on their own when public support is high, elite allies are willing to offer support, and multiple pathways are open to influence change legislatively and culturally (Balser 1997). In this way, a plentiful environment, with high levels of public support, will lower pressure on organizational factions to resolve internal disputes. Theoretically, these conditions should mean that there are more organizational splits during times of social movement growth.

If expanding movements result in more splits, contracting movements should have the effect of keeping factions inside their parent longer (cf. Shriver and Messer 2009). When the larger movement is contracting and fewer available resources are up for grabs, factions likely recognize their reduced chances of surviving if they were to break away. In this case, there is greater incentive to reconcile differences and to stay (McCarthy and Zald 1977). However, the relationship between movement decline and organizational splitting has important caveats. It can be difficult to predict exactly how factions will respond to a reduction in resources. Fewer available resources may just delay the envitable break, meaning longer and more acrimonious fights before factions ultimately split. The relationship also likely depends on the reason for movement decline. State repression often leads to movement decline, and particular organizations may split over how to respond to these threats (Balser 1997; Shriver and Messer 2009).

Time Period—Issue Connection

As I noted earlier, even in generalist organizations that embrace dozens of issues at any given time, some issues are prioritized and others are marginalized. Activists working on prioritized issues will enjoy greater resources and attention, while those working on peripheral issues will get markedly less. Because resources are finite, there will always be more marginalized issues than there are prioritized issues. But the issues themselves are not permanently fixed in one location or the other. Previously peripheralized issues might gain traction for any number of reasons—including increased public concern, new legislation, or a high-profile news event. At these times, leaders may elect to reshuffle organizational priorities, moving some issues from the core into more peripheral locations so that money and attention can be redirected to rising issues.

The time period–issue connection can work in unpredictable ways. Sometimes an emerging issue will be so urgent that organizations might split off new groups intentionally as a way to attract coalition partners or funding to support it. At other times, it might simply usurp resources from other issue areas, factionalizing activists working on the marginalized task forces.

Developed Infrastructure

Decentralized bureaucracies are organized to include multiple levels. Federated organizations often include national, regional, state, and local levels. More levels means that factions have more places in which to carry out their fights, even after losing some battles (King 2008). Less developed organizational infrastructure means factions have fewer options for continuing. Theoretically, this means that organizations with fewer levels should experience more organizational splitting. Organizations with more developed infrastructure will be better able to maintain factions without splitting because factions generally have more options in choosing to stay.

Elaborate infrastructure also means that factions operating at the bureaucratic core will have the greatest power to move their fights to different parts of the organization. Factions starting from lower positions have much less freedom to expand their fights to new levels of the organization. Taken together, we can hypothesize that organizations with fewer levels and less developed infrastructure will experience more organizational splitting. In those groups with highly developed infrastructure, factions that emerge at the bottom should be more likely to eventually break away. NOW's history of splitting seems to bear out this pattern.

Conclusion

Conflict in social movements is unavoidable, and we have no shortage of academic literature theorizing its emergence and its consequences. And yet this literature has been strangely quiet about the factionalism that develops in the largest and best-known social movement organizations. Bureaucratic groups are the mainstays in movements, persisting even in hostile political and cultural moments. Their stability and durability have blinded us to the ways they experience the same conflicts that roil the smaller collectives.

Not only do bureaucratic groups experience conflict but their structures make particular kinds of splitting likely. By paying attention to the ways bureaucratic structures create and bind subgroups of members, we are better able to see how organizations like NOW can be stable and durable while also experiencing repeated episodes of factionalization and schism. By clarifying how and why these bureaucratic factions emerge, we are also able to see the generative energy and creativity that flow from these conflicts. Bureaucratic organizations are not just workhorses for the movements they inhabit; they are also important generators of movement theory and ideologies.

Paying attention to the ways conflict is generated in bureaucratic organizations reveals how many splits happen without rancorous fighting or fireworks. Instead, many splits develop slowly and simmer for long periods before factions ease away from the parent, careful to maintain working partnerships toward common goals. These are often less dramatic stories than the ones we usually tell about schisms, but they are also much more common. In the following chapters, I detail the emergence of factionalism across NOW's peripheral and core locations, including its local chapters, its national board of directors, its task forces and committees, and its satellite organizations. Each location has a unique mix of tensions between freedom and power that shapes members' decisions about breaking away from NOW.

CHAPTER THREE

Breaking at the Roots

Local Schism in NOW

When Betty Boyer stood to leave the second annual NOW conference in 1967, she already had an inkling that she would not be back for the next one. NOW members at the conference, mostly from the East Coast, had voted to support the repeal of all abortion restrictions. As a national board member representing the Ohio chapters she had personally organized, Boyer knew in her gut that this was not a position that her local chapters would accept. The Ohio recruits were conservative—at least more conservative than NOW members from the East Coast—and they were deeply private about all sexual issues, including the need for abortion services. Boyer saw the problem as a strategic one; the Midwest women she had recruited would flee NOW, and likely the whole movement, when they learned about the abortion position. But the midwestern chapters were smaller and less powerful than the East Coast chapters that had pushed for it. In a rational calculation, she understood that conservative chapters were simply unlikely to win in a direct battle over the issue. With a small cadre of Ohio members, Boyer walked out of the conference in protest. It would take nearly a year, but Boyer's faction exited NOW completely to found the Women's Equity Action League (WEAL), a "conservative NOW" that focused more narrowly on educational and institutional discrimination against women (Costain and Costain 1987).

Just a year later, New York City NOW, its largest and most politically radical chapter, endured its own split when a small group of members tried and failed to bring in the organizing strategies they had learned in the new left and women's liberation groups. Led by Ti-Grace Atkinson, the faction sought to dismantle the elected positions in the chapter and replace them with a lot system in which all members took turns being leaders. Making a case for the collectivist structures of the women's liberation branch, they argued that genuine feminism required egalitarian power arrangements, with no member exercising authority over others. NOW's existing system of elected officers and a board of directors violated these principles and should be changed to reflect members' inherent equality. In a viciously contested election in 1968, Atkinson's faction lost and immediately split from NOW to form the October 17 Movement, named for the day of the lost election. They later renamed themselves simply "The Feminists."

Both WEAL and The Feminists started as local contingents of NOW, and both were shaped by the local communities outside of NOW. In the Midwest, many of the women who joined the movement remained religious and culturally conservative. They advocated for women's educational and legal equality but were uncomfortable with the radical social values bubbling in other parts of NOW and the broader feminist movement. Especially on the East Coast, activists raced ahead on social issues, challenging marriage, heterosexuality, capitalism, religion, and standard organizational forms. Especially in the early years of the second-wave feminist movement, these distinct styles of activism could coexist in the same movement without deleterious effects. In fact, scholars have found myriad ways that diversity in both goals and tactics within a movement can help the whole achieve more than would have been possible with a singular approach (Haines 1984; McCammon, Bergner, and Arch 2015; Levitsky 2007; Wang and Soule 2012). Diversity, however, is much more difficult to manage within organizations than between them. Because of NOW's wide geographical reach, every possible way of doing feminism seeped into the organization, challenging leaders to balance all of the diversity in the movement with one set of coherent organizational practices. Boyer's and Atkinson's factions provide two examples of the struggle for localized feminism in a bureaucratic national organization.

As with other formalized organizations, conventional wisdom holds that NOW was good at managing diversity because members enjoyed a great deal of freedom at the local level, with only minimal restrictions coming from the national leaders. In describing the relationship between NOW's core leaders at the national level and its local activists, early NOW member Minnie Bruce Pratt (2005) remembers NOW's chapters as sites of creative and distinctive activism: "NOW chapters were really more wild and woolly than NOW proper [national NOW], because it was just groups of women who needed some kind of affiliation to do stuff. . . . We were doing all kinds of local organizing."

In theory, this is just how decentralized bureaucracies should work. NOW is often used as the primary example of how the liberal feminists in the bureaucratic branch of the movement avoided the crippling factionalism that plagued small, collective groups (Staggenborg 1989; Reger 2002a). As discussed in chapter 2, small, single-tiered groups worked well when they were limited to the women who already knew each other and were friends before joining the groups. As they grew beyond the initial core group of friends, collectives often struggled to accommodate diversity while maintaining the same level of trust required for consensus decision-making (Polletta 2002). In contrast, liberal feminists used their experiences in government agencies, corporations, universities, and unions to build elaborate organizations with multiple tiers, leadership elections, and term limits that minimized and channeled conflict among members (Mueller 1995). While the national administration is tightly governed by written rules and procedures for decision-making and task delegation, local members enjoy a great deal of freedom to organize themselves however they want. From the outset, NOW chapters took their freedom seriously, and local chapters reflected the distinct circumstances of their communities (Reger and Staggenborg 2006; Turk 2010). This balance of power, accountability, and autonomy provides NOW, and organizations like it, with stability through rules, procedures, and structure as well as protection against schism.

The federated form allowed members to create internal communities with their own distinct collective identities within the larger national structure (Reger and Staggenborg 2006). Pockets of autonomy and independence allowed these subcommunities to do feminism in the ways they wanted, *almost* regardless of what the national organization was doing. They could focus on particular issues and projects that were meaningful to them while maintaining the benefits of membership in a large, well-known, and comparatively powerful national organization. By any measure, this approach is laudable, and it likely attracted many women who would not have joined NOW otherwise. Their freedom reduced members' discontent because they enjoyed the perks of being associated with a nationally known organization while still enjoying high degrees of autonomy. Members pursued the projects and strategies they preferred, focusing on their own communities in the ways that resonated locally.

Yet, schisms like Boyer's and Atkinson's call this conventional wisdom into question. The differences between NOW's core and its grassroots chapters created a mismatch in many places between the evolving local identities and NOW's national brand. As John McCarthy (2005) has noted, there is no shortage of conflict between local and national levels in federated groups, including the balance of power among the organizational levels; member loyalty to the local group over the national organization; territorial disputes with other local chapters; financial support and control; and the selection of goals, tactics, and procedures. Both Boyer's and Atkinson's disputes fell into these well-established categories. But the bureaucratic form should have enabled compromises to resolve their disputes. Boyer's faction could have remained focused on the issues they cared about most, like women's education equality; Atkinson's faction could have taken the same route that the Berkeley chapter had taken, which was to ignore the formal rules and rotate the leadership positions however they wished.

But these compromises weren't viable in the eyes of the members involved. In their individual chapters, whatever freedom they had from national mandates couldn't outweigh the burden of NOW's identity in their local context. They lacked the resources and capacity to change the national organization (Zald and Berger 1978), and they were forced to choose between the benefits of NOW membership and their localized beliefs for what it meant to be a good feminist. While NOW has done a remarkable job in retaining and recruiting members since its founding, its chapters have often served as incubators for member schisms when the gap between their local contexts and their national organization's is too wide. This is surprising, and indicates that we should revisit the well-worn argument that formalization reins in factionalism.

Revising the Branched View of American Feminism

The American feminist movement is frequently framed as divided into two distinct branches. On one side, young feminists formed small, unstable collectives; the other side was filled with large, formalized bureaucracies. Jo Freeman (1975, 2000) argued that the "younger" (radical) branch and the "older" (liberal) branch of the feminist movement often had trouble working together, despite sharing many goals, because they used different external reference points in evaluating which goals women should be chasing and how their organizations should work. The younger branch looked to other radical movements from which they had come, leading them to value consensus-based decision-making in small collectives. In contrast, the older liberal feminists referred to the professional and business organizations in which they had served to build their feminist groups. Liberal feminists built bureaucratic structures that were durable and better equipped to withstand the ebbs and flows of public support for the movement. But, as Freeman also notes, their distinct preferences also intersected inside of feminist organizations, as younger women migrated into NOW from the liberation branch over time.

Moreover, NOW's members were not simply middle-of-the-road moderates. They were a true cross section of feminism's wide diversity in ideology and style. Because it was one of the few national organizations, NOW was often the only feminist group in local communities (Gilmore 2013). Particularly at the local level, there was no clear line delineating liberal from radical feminism; many of the same activists populated both kinds of groups, often simultaneously. Personal relationships and friendships threaded the two kinds of feminism closer together and facilitated the flow of ideas from the small groups into NOW's universe. Ideologies developed in the movement's radical wing showed up in local NOW chapters, leading to a struggle between their local values and those of the national leaders. Of course, many local activists did work their way up NOW's chain, starting in chapters and graduating over time to the regional and national boards, where they might more directly affect the culture and structure of the organization. But there is a selection effect at work in this trajectory: the leaders who made these leaps, perhaps being more amenable to bureaucratic life, were also likely to be different from those who stayed in the organization's local periphery.

NOW's federated structure makes it difficult for dissenting local members to be heard at higher levels of the organization, leaving them with few options beyond accepting what they don't like or leaving to form a new group (Zald and Berger 1978; Liebman, Sutton, and Wuthnow 1988). Many local NOW factions have chosen the latter route. This was certainly true for chapters with deep roots in radical feminism, but it was also true for more conservative chapters, filled with women deeply uncomfortable with what they perceived to be the confrontational and radical actions of NOW chapters in geographically and culturally distant places. Over time, national NOW tried to balance the competing, and often incompatible, interests of its diverse membership, but it is impossible to meet every demand from chapters in such a large and diverse organization.

Regional Differences in NOW and the Creation of Schisms

When its founders announced that they were starting NOW, they were surprised and overwhelmed by the immediate outpouring of support from women and men all over the country. Thousands of eager recruits flocked to NOW in its first year, wanting to become members, form chapters, and start campaigns against women's inequality. NOW members varied tremendously in the issues they cared about and how they wanted to tackle them. In response, NOW founders created a loose structure that allowed members to pursue whatever projects they found meaningful. Local chapters were given free rein to determine their own priorities, drawn from "any subject which is directly related to the purpose of NOW" (quoted from Turk 2010). Indeed, local leaders used this freedom as a selling point in recruiting new members. A founding chapter leader from New Jersey recalled that she would assure skeptical newcomers that "they weren't buying into a whole package. They could devote their efforts to something they believed in" (quoted in Davis 1999, 58).

On one hand, the immense freedom at the chapter level allowed a variety of feminisms to flourish within NOW. On the other hand, it caused conflict when the local feminist identities clashed with the reputation and priorities of national NOW (Gilmore 2013; Kretschmer 2014; Reger and Staggenborg 2006). Gene Boyer (1991), a NOW founder and board member from Wisconsin, recalls how difficult it was to keep chapters going in her home state:

> I must say that many of them had to be started two or three times. . . .
> Every time I would get it started and go off to a national convention,
> I would come back to find I didn't have any members left because of
> what they'd just read in the paper about the organization adopting a
> lesbian resolution or confronting this person or that one.

Chapters from conservative regions balked at being a part of an organization that made the news for its extreme stances. Members from progressive areas were often frustrated by the slow pace of activism and what they perceived as the conservative orientation of the national leaders.

Most chapters found ways to manage the gap between their local context and national NOW's reputation. In these chapters, members accepted NOW's broader limitations and managed to use local connections to develop new, external organizations that would meet their goals, while they maintained their NOW memberships. These were not schisms, per se; members simply did both kinds of organizing at the same time, seeing the new group as an extension of their NOW work. In her study of NOW's chapter activism, Stephanie Gilmore (2013) reported that Memphis NOW members joined forces with a variety of other local groups, including Church Women United, the League of Women Voters, and the local YWCA to create the Women's Resource Center. The Center provided social services to Memphis women where their needs were not being met by local agencies. In another case, chapter president Shelley Fernandez and a small group of San Francisco NOW members established Casa De Las Madres, a shelter for battered women and their children. The idea was born in the chapter's Consciousness Raising Committee, and NOW members staffed the organization for several years. Despite the connection between the chapter and the shelter, Fernandez and the cofounders incorporated it and raised money for it separately from NOW (S. Fernandez, telephone interview with the author, March 1, 2010). National NOW's emphasis on structural and political outcomes left little room for these kinds of direct services to local women. This mismatch between national NOW and their local priorities led many chapters to work outside of NOW to bridge the gap between what they could accomplish as a NOW chapter and what they wanted to do in their communities.

While many factions found this sort of compromise to be a viable path for staying in NOW, other factions were unable to integrate their localized feminism with NOW's national agenda. These conflicts are often provoked by two related forces: cultural differences across the organization, and the effect of local connections on the way factions came to understand the national organization. Occurring across the radical–conservative spectrum, these cases demonstrate how the same characteristics that make nationally federated organizations so durable can also turn chapters into incubators of factionalism and schism.

Forming the Women's Equity Action League

Nowhere is the tension between NOW's national collective identity and the local feminist context more apparent than in the formation of Boyer's WEAL. Even before the 1967 second annual national conference, the differences between the midwestern chapters and coastal chapters were apparent. East Coast chapters openly advocated for pushing NOW in a more radical direction, especially on abortion rights issues, which were central to their understanding of feminism. They were aware of the possible fallout of this decision; in her notes describing the meeting, Jean Faust, a board member from New York, wrote:

> We knew that many members were afraid of supporting abortion
> rights—both because they were not accustomed to discussing private
> matters in public and because they felt emotional arguments over
> this subject would alienate women whose support we needed for

educational and employment opportunities. (National Organization for Women Records 1967b)

Despite the misgivings of conservative chapters, New York members pushed the issue at the conference and the motion in support of abortion rights passed by 57 to 14; roughly one-third of those in attendance refused to cast a vote (National Organization for Women Records 1967b).

In contrast to the more radically oriented chapters in the East, the local chapters Boyer had organized were filled with "older women, professionals, other lawyers, women she knew, her own nieces, and friends of friends" (Paterson 1986, 175). NOW had been getting increasingly negative press, and Boyer believed that it needed women whom the media "couldn't lay a glove on" (Paterson 1986, 175). Conservative and moderate women would be more difficult for elites and the broader public to dismiss, and if NOW wanted to keep these women, it needed to convince them that the organization would represent their sensibilities as well. When the news broke that national NOW had declared its support for abortion rights, Boyer understood that the mainstream and conservative women she had worked so hard to recruit would refuse to join local NOW chapters, even if those local chapters stayed away from the issue. Worse yet, given NOW's prominence in the burgeoning feminist movement, the decision might keep otherwise sympathetic women away from the movement completely.

But the choice to leave NOW was not simple. NOW's growing power both culturally and politically meant that leaving the organization would mean sacrificing this influence. A new organization would also mean starting from scratch. Upon returning to Ohio, Boyer called an emergency meeting to ask members what they wanted to do. She first offered a "stay and fight" option to put pressure on NOW to drop the abortion issue. It was, after all, a democratic organization, and there was a small chance that conservative chapters might be able to hold off, or even roll back, the abortion stance before it caused too much trouble. Boyer also offered the option to split away from NOW and form a different organization that would "proceed along the original lines of NOW" (Women's Equity Action League Records 1967a). Ohio members responded as Boyer suspected they would; they wanted a new organization that would represent women's educational and employment interests without touching controversial issues like abortion.

In early 1968, Boyer announced her decision to start a new organization that would represent a moderate perspective in the feminist movement (National Organization for Women Records 1968a). WEAL declared that it would not seek to undermine NOW but instead work to recruit women who would not "feel at home in NOW." Staying true to its commitment to stay away from divisive cultural issues, WEAL's founding documents make no mention of abortion at all (Women's Equity Action League Records 1967b). It was initially designed as a state organization that would stay local to Ohio (Disney and Gelb 2000). By 1981, it had moved to lobbying at the national level for educational and employment equality. Ironically, it also declared a position in favor of abortion rights by the early 1970s, as reproductive rights became a central pillar of the feminist movement (Kretschmer 2014).

Forming The Feminists

While the midwestern chapters of NOW were filled with conservative women who sometimes resented the power of East Coast members to dictate the organization's agenda, the East Coast chapters, particularly in the Northeast, were filled with women whose feminism had been shaped by the radical ideology of the women's liberation wing. NOW's New York City chapter, its first and largest, was also its most radical (Echols 1989). Many New York City members simultaneously participated in both NOW and the radical groups forming around the city; they created a bridge between the wings of the movement, carrying radical values and ideologies into the NOW chapter.

The fight over liberal and radical ideologies first came to a head in the New York City chapter when Ti-Grace Atkinson, a graduate student from Columbia and an active participant in the student movement on that campus, joined NOW in 1967 (Eastwood 1992). At the behest of Betty Friedan, Atkinson also joined the national board of directors because Friedan believed that her Republican connections and good looks would help lure in financial donations (Friedan 2000). Their relationship abruptly soured, as Atkinson, who had become the president of the New York City chapter, began advocating for a variety of divisive issues in NOW, including pressing for the organization to support abortion rights (National Organization for Women Records 1968b), incorporation of a dues structure in which poorer women would not have to pay for membership, and the dissolution of leadership positions altogether (Paterson 1986). According to Jean Faust (1990), Atkinson's leadership decisions were shaped by the external groups to which she was connected: "She got involved with a group of radical students who decided that we [NOW] weren't radical enough. They wanted to make us more radical." Rather than elected positions, Atkinson proposed "the elimination of all offices" and that the organization "operate on the level of committees, the chairs of which would rotate and be chosen by lot from the general membership" (Mary O. Eastwood Papers 1968, 1970a, 1970b). Along with a handful of members, Atkinson wanted to implement this system in the New York chapter of NOW.

Because Atkinson's faction was looking to formally change the bylaws by which the largest chapter in the organization operated, rather than implementing the lot system informally, she faced heavy opposition from the national board, particularly from its Legal Committee. The Legal Committee was responsible for ensuring that NOW abided by government regulations for nonprofit organizations. The organization had already been incorporated with the IRS with a mandated leadership structure. While the hierarchical structure was unacceptable to Atkinson's faction in New York, it was not negotiable for national NOW leaders, who wanted to retain the benefits of state recognition (National Organization for Women Records 1968b; McCarthy, Britt, and Wolfson 1991).

Beyond logistical differences, there were deeper identity differences between Atkinson's New York faction and national NOW. National leaders believed that a hierarchical structure was critical for accomplishing legal and political goals. From this viewpoint, the purpose of the organization was to obtain tangible economic and political gains for women. These gains, they argued, could only come through hierarchical structures in which responsibility would be carried by a few dedicated leaders (National Organization for Women Records 1968b). While local factions held the same priorities—economic and political equality for women— their common goals were refracted through a local understanding of what it meant be good feminists. Using hierarchical structures was fundamentally at odds with the New York faction's sense of feminism, and they would not agree to compromises that kept these structures in place, even just in name.

Undeterred by the opposition from national leaders, Atkinson brought the bylaws proposal to a vote on October 17, 1968, in the New York chapter. Everyone involved in the meeting agreed that the proposal was defeated by a wide margin, but how this outcome emerged is a matter of debate. According to national NOW leaders, Atkinson's bylaws were defeated 44 to 18 in a routine election (M. Fox, telephone interview with the author, June 1, 2009). Atkinson (1974, 68) understood the election differently, casting it as an undemocratic battle waged by national NOW leaders against her chapter's local autonomy:

> The rest of the officers in NOW banded together to defeat the [bylaws] by packing the meeting and buying up votes in the worst American tradition. Moving speeches were presented castigating me as an unnatural traitor to my class and appealing to the great American dream (or nightmare, depending on your view).

For Atkinson, the results of the election represented not just an organizational defeat but also evidence that NOW's formalized bureaucratic structure would never be a vehicle for the radical values she had developed through contact with women's liberation and students' rights groups. She perceived the loss in New York as proof that other NOW leaders were imitating the same oppressive system that she wanted to destroy. Atkinson (1974, 10–11) explained this position in her resignation letter:

> I am resigning my offices because . . . I realize that by holding these offices I am participating in oppression itself. You cannot destroy oppression by filling the position of the oppressor. I don't think you can fight oppression "from the inside"; you either are on the inside or the outside and you fill one of these two ranks by your presence. Since I have failed to get rid of the power positions I hold, I have no choice but to step out of them.

Ti-Grace Atkinson believed that NOW could not be revolutionary if it remained hierarchically organized. When she could not change its structure, she opted to leave it completely. Named for the day of the lost election, Atkinson and a small group of members left NOW to form a new organization, originally called the October 17 Movement and later renamed "The Feminists," that would fit their vision of what feminism should be.

In explaining their decision to break away from NOW, members of The Feminists wrote essays using the language of the local women's liberation movement. They explained:

> We have seen how the hierarchical-type structure, as exemplified in the National Organization for Women, concentrates the power and initiative at the top with the broad base of the general membership bearing the load. . . . In The Feminists there are no permanent officers: A different chairwoman is chosen by lot for each meeting, no person taking a second turn until all members have chaired. . . . In this way

tyranny by any one person does not develop and no one comes to be identified with a position of power. (Mary O. Eastwood Papers 1968, 1970a, 1970b)

After the split, NOW's decentralized bureaucratic structure guaranteed that leaders would continue to tolerate, even encourage, significant variation in how its members understood feminism, while Atkinson's new group insisted on a strict definition of what feminism meant and adopted stringent membership rules. Over time, The Feminists' extreme standards for appropriate behavior and ideology were too much for most members to abide, and many cut their ties completely with the group. The Feminists lasted a few years after splitting from NOW but had disbanded completely by 1973 (Echols 1989).

Of course, local factions don't always make this choice. In 1970, another group of New York City NOW members sought to bring into NOW the values of radical feminism, this time in the form of consciousness-raising, or "rapping" (Reger 2002a). NOW leaders produced a structural compromise in the form of a consciousness-raising subcommittee that would be free from the hierarchical structures of the rest of the chapter. This episode of factionalism had a happy ending, with the Consciousness Raising Committee serving as an important site of recruiting and educating new NOW members, who would often then cycle into the other committees. In this case, the decentralized bureaucratic form allowed leaders to reach a compromise, retaining space for local diversity and avoiding a schism.

Lesbian Factionalism in NOW

Regional and local differences also shaped how chapters related to national NOW around cultural issues. No issue better exemplifies this chasm than lesbianism in NOW's early years. Many in NOW feared that an open acknowledgment of and discussion about lesbianism would undermine the movement—Betty Friedan famously referred to lesbians as the "lavender menace." National leaders actively avoided lesbian rights discussions, even as the New York City chapter began to fold the issue into its agenda (Echols 1989). Shortly after NOW's founding, New York leader Ivy Bottini organized a consciousness-raising session devoted to the question "Is Lesbianism a Feminist Issue?" and Rita Mae Brown, who joined NOW in 1969 after short stints in the civil rights movement and the burgeoning gay liberation movement, used her position on the New York chapter newsletter to advocate for lesbian rights. By 1970, in what's become known as the lesbian purge, Brown was fired from her post as newsletter editor and she left NOW with a small group of other NOW lesbians. In their subsequent statement detailing their experiences in NOW, they outlined the essential problems between their local faction and the preferences of the national leaders they had fought:

> Lesbian is the one word that can cause the Executive Committee a collective heart attack. This issue is dismissed as unimportant, too dangerous to contemplate, divisive or whatever the excuse could be dredged up from their repression. The prevailing attitude is, and this reflected even more on the national level, "suppose they . . . flock to us in droves? How horrible. After all, think of our image." (quoted from Marotta 1981, 235)

The purge continued as Friedan, with help from other NOW leaders, successfully blocked any other lesbians from being elected or reelected to NYC NOW in the 1970 elections. It remained a sticking point between lesbian activists scattered across local chapters and national leaders until mid-1971, when, at the annual conference, members passed a resolution to support lesbianism as a legal and moral right.

After national NOW took a position in support of lesbian rights as a fundamental feminist concern, conservative members in local NOW chapters were forced to reconsider their memberships. Embedded in a conservative community in a southern state, straight women in NOW's Memphis chapter grew increasingly anxious about lesbians in the years following national NOW's shift. Unable to reconcile their identities with the national NOW's embrace of lesbian rights, a faction of straight women broke away in 1982, opting to revive a chapter of the Memphis Women's Political Caucus. In their new group, the former NOW members focused solely on women's political representation and avoided the politics of sexuality completely. The faction saw distancing themselves from NOW as a necessary step "if they wanted to retain a political voice in the city" (Gilmore 2013, 66).

In each of these cases, locally rooted communities in NOW were a generative and creative force in feminism, even as they came into direct conflict with NOW's national identity and style of feminism. Sometimes this resulted in splits that filled out the radical side of the feminist movement. Sometimes they broke in conservative directions, giving women with more traditional values a place to plug in to the movement. In each case, the schism resulted in an independent local group that was a better match for its local community than a NOW-affiliated group could be.

For such a large and geographically dispersed organization, it's difficult to imagine how schisms could be avoided, or even that they should be avoided. Members will always be influenced by their local cultures in ways that make them different from members in other, far-flung chapters. When conflicts emerged, the federated structure made it difficult for local dissenters to remake national NOW in ways that would allow them to stay. They had immense freedom to do as they wished locally but little power to make other units of NOW fall in line with their vision. The benefit of NOW's prominence in the movement wasn't enough for these factions to stay when they could forge a new organization that better matched their local culture and values. In the next section, I explore a different dimension of how local chapters incubate schisms by focusing more explicitly on how external local networks affect how NOW members understand their organization.

Local Connections and Breaking Away

The roots of schism in local chapters often begin not with internal conflict but with external bridges that bring new ideas into the chapter. Just as Bruno Dyck and Frederick A. Starke (1999, 803) found in their work on schism in religious organizations, members who broke away from NOW often did so after being exposed to and then adopting new ideas that were inconsistent with the rest of their organization. Particularly in the 1970s, the feminist universe was bubbling with different strains of feminism, including liberal feminism, represented by NOW, but also socialist, radical, and cultural feminisms. Socialist feminism emerged from and remained connected to the new left, emphasizing how class inequality was tied to gender inequality (Echols 1989). Radical feminism brought enormous energy and innovation into the movement by experimenting with new organizational forms, styles of leadership, and gender theories. Radical feminism presented the cutting edge of the movement; its groups were the first to demand a repeal of abortion restrictions, greater access to safe contraception, and child care centers and the first to publicly and unapologetically critique "family, marriage, love, normative heterosexuality, and rape" (Echols 1989, 3–4). They also created new strategies for bringing social change, including the use of consciousness-raising groups that helped women connect their private experiences to systemic oppression.

As radical feminism was cresting, cultural feminism began to build momentum. Cultural feminists understood gender differences as innate, essential, and positive. Women, they argued, are superior to men because their biology makes them "closer to nature" as well as "nurturant, loving, and egalitarian" (Echols 1983, 38). According to cultural feminists, patriarchy undervalued women's reproductive powers, creating a sense even among women that their bodies should be controlled and managed to maximize their similarity to men. Instead, women should be committed to maintaining gender differences and valorizing the traits that make women different from men (Alcoff 1988).

As radical and cultural strains of feminism grew, debates about what counts as "good" feminism increased in NOW as well. The federated structure of NOW made these localized conflicts impossible to avoid. Individual chapters are shaped not just by the people who join but also by the relationships members forge in their local communities. When there were multiple feminist groups in a community or geographical area, women didn't always choose only one but held multiple memberships. They did so for many reasons—often because different groups focused on different things or because their friends were members of a range of groups. These members carried ideas and values across organizational boundaries. At other times, the values they encounter in another part of the community might lead a member to begin questioning NOW or even pressing for those values to be adopted in NOW. These networks sometimes created factionalism in NOW chapters, and local connections also made it easier for some factions to break away.

Forming Feminists for Life

Patricia Goltz was initially drawn to NOW after reading Betty Friedan's book *The Feminine Mystique*. In 1970, she began attending the Columbus, Ohio, NOW chapter meetings. At roughly the same time she was considering joining, she learned that the organization held a pro-choice position. Despite her misgivings about its reproductive rights stance, she agreed with the rest of NOW's agenda and decided she would devote her effort to NOW's other projects. Goltz even began recruiting other women to NOW, including Cathy Callahan, a friend from her Judo class. According to Goltz, Callahan had been reluctant to join NOW or the mainstream feminist movement because she felt it was "playing on the weaknesses of women" rather than emphasizing their inherent strengths. Goltz convinced her to start coming to the NOW meetings by arguing that the movement needed women like her to make it better.

In 1972, Goltz and Callahan came to the same conclusion that Betty Boyer, of WEAL, had come to four years earlier: the feminist movement needed space for conservative and moderate women. They also embraced a cultural feminist orientation, arguing that women's capacity to bear children was an important trait to be valued, not undermined with reproductive rights rhetoric. While maintaining their membership in NOW, they decided to form a small, local, and relatively informal organization that would create space for an anti-abortion position with feminist logic. Callahan served as the financial backer, and Goltz operated as the organization's public face. After a local Columbus newspaper covered their new organization, Goltz was regularly invited to speak by local pro-life groups, helping Feminists for Life (FFL) recruit new supporters and members, particularly from religious communities.

Goltz and Callahan were influenced by radical and cultural feminist frames that emphasize women's reproductive and nurturing capacities. In its early years, when Goltz and Callahan were still members of NOW, many of FFL's members identified as a part of the radical movement and wanted to be a part of an organization that prioritized women's spiritual and biological connections to children (R. MacNair, telephone interview with the author, November 16, 2009). These members provided a niche for FFL in the broader feminist movement. But as the years wore on, cultural feminism declined, and FFL leaders had an easier time recruiting support from conservative religious pro-life activists and organizations than it did from feminist activists. The post–*Roe v. Wade* pro-life movement was filling with religious women who had a special interest in validating women's experiences as mothers (Luker 1985). This demographic shift gave FFL a bridge into the religious pro-life movement, which provided legitimacy to the organization that other local feminist groups increasingly refused. Devout women made up a large part of FFL's early recruits, and it was primarily Catholic members who pulled FFL further into the religious pro-life movement. While the new members were helpful in bringing in resources, they were also less interested in maintaining a place in the feminist movement.

FFL originally tried to resist spilling over to the religious right movement. But, according to Goltz, FFL's efforts to distance from the religious pro-life movement and to pursue relationships within the feminist movement were "a waste of time" (P. Goltz, telephone interview with the author, December 4, 2009). The pro-life movement offered ample opportunities for FFL's participation in their campaigns and conferences because pro-life activists saw utility in having feminists on their side of the abortion debate. Each of the FFL leaders I interviewed named the National Right to Life Committee (NRLC) as its main coalition partner.

The U.S. Conference of Catholic Bishops (USCCB) formed the NRLC in 1971 to build a social movement in support of pro-life beliefs (Hanna 1979; McKeegan 1992; Staggenborg 1991). It remains the largest pro-life organization in the United States. The relationship between FFL and NRLC developed early in both organizations' histories. Despite NRLC's initial suspicions of a feminist group, FFL was a frequent supporter of its local chapters. Goltz (2009) recalls:

> They held those [NRLC board] meetings and I asked if we could come and they let us come, and at first they thought we were spies. . . . But when they did understand that we were on their side, then we always had the opportunity to give a report each month at that meeting. And they would inform people that they knew would be interested in the organization about us and then those people would get in touch.

The relationship between the two local organizations expanded to the national level. In an interview with the author, FFL leader Rosemary Oelrich Bottcher (telephone interview with the author, November 4, 2009) reflected on the relationship between FFL and the religious anti-abortion movement: "The National Right to Life Committee was very interested in what we had to say, and printed a lot of my articles, and I did a lot of book reviews for them, and we were invited to their conferences to speak and give workshops."

In the early 1970s, the Feminists for Life faction tried to maintain bridges between its cultural feminist members, NOW, and the growing number of religious supporters. But support for abortion rights had become settled dogma in the feminist movement, and the differences across these diverse groups became too difficult to ignore. In late 1973, the Columbus NOW chapter leaders began proceedings to revoke Goltz's membership, and they formally expelled her from the local chapter in 1974. They did not move to expel Callahan, however, and Goltz could have maintained her membership in national NOW. But both women, along with one other chapter member, left the organization completely. The local community of pro-life activists had provided FFL with a membership base and an organizational life outside of NOW, and the ideology of these religious connections shifted FFL in more conservative directions (Kretschmer 2014).

Forming National Women's Liberation

While overlapping memberships pulled FFL faction members toward cultural feminism and religious conservatism, other chapters were pulled toward the radical branch of the movement. Beginning in the mid-1990s, a group of Gainesville, Florida, NOW members grew concerned that NOW was neglecting the priorities important to younger women. The Gainesville chapter had a significant overlap with both the University of Florida campus NOW chapter and another local feminist group called Gainesville Women's Liberation (GWL), which focused on educating college students about the principles of radical feminism. Campus NOW, Gainesville Area NOW, and GWL co-sponsored local events, including protests directed at the student health service on campus for making it difficult for female students to obtain the morning-after pill (also commonly known as emergency contraception). Women who held simultaneous memberships in these groups carried the more radical ideologies from GWL into the NOW chapters, facilitating the sense among NOW activists that national leaders were not pressing for a truly radical agenda.

In June 2000, GWL hosted a course on women's liberation followed by a consciousness-raising session attended by several local NOW members. As a part of the session, Gainesville NOW members aired their frustration over the gap between the radical feminist principles they valued locally and what they saw from national NOW leaders. Rather than empowering the grass roots, Gainesville NOW members had begun to feel that national NOW was operating as a "public relations or lobbying force" (C. Churchill, interview with the author, July 6, 2009). They feared that national NOW was including too many issues in the organizational agenda and devoting too many resources to lobbying instead of prioritizing the issues that would improve real women's lives, like abortion rights, birth control, and child care (*Gainesville NOW Newsletter* 2000).

Women who held simultaneous memberships in both groups carried the more radical ideologies from GWL into Gainesville NOW. To reconcile these conflicting approaches to feminism, Gainesville NOW members tried in a variety of ways to press national NOW into a more aggressive political stance. At the 2000 NOW national conference, roughly twelve Gainesville members interrupted a plenary session to protest what they perceived to be NOW's conservative agenda. They marched around the conference hall carrying signs and inviting other NOW members to join their movement. The faction was able to gain enough signatures to get their proposals on the ballot, but NOW leaders put the proposals at the bottom of the agenda, effectively burying them, and the issue never reached a vote. The faction's perception of what happened at the conference reflects what Austin Choi-Fitzpatrick (2015) describes as the scripting and managing of the organizational decision-making by leaders to bolster the appearance of democracy while shutting out inconvenient ideas. Whether this was national NOW's intention matters less than the fact that this is what the faction believes happened. They were disillusioned by NOW leaders' refusal to take their proposals seriously, and it cast doubt on whether they could have a meaningful place in the larger organization. The message they took away was that NOW was not the right organization for a group like theirs or for their ideas.

Following the conference, the Gainesville faction refocused their efforts on increasing access to reproductive services in their local area, in particular, at the University of Florida. But in 2005, the faction recognized an opportunity to take their local fight back to the national level. They organized a sit-in protest at the Federal Drug Administration (FDA) headquarters to draw attention to the FDA's foot dragging about making the morning-after pill available over the counter (Kaufman 2005). The faction reached out to national NOW for support, but NOW leaders responded by telling the Gainesville members to go home. According to Candi Churchill, they were told, "You can't park anywhere, you're all going to be thrown in jail, you shouldn't do this; this will make us look bad." This rejection was the final straw for the group, and its members began planning to form a new organization.

In June 2009, the faction launched National Women's Liberation (NWL). The decision to break away was a long time in coming, as the members weighed their desire to build a group that fit their identity against their loyalty to NOW. Churchill described the struggle this way:

> I would say we've really been working on it very hard for maybe three years. Before that it was like, "What are we doing in NOW? Is this making a difference? Do we keep organizing in NOW?" And the answer was usually yes, because what else are you going to do?

By asking "what else are you going to do?" Churchill implied the dilemma of accepting their peripheral isolation from the powerful national organization versus the risk of starting a competing group. NOW's reputation and influence are unparalleled in the feminist movement, and few other organizations can compete with it for members, resources, and attention. These qualities kept the Gainesville members from breaking away from NOW for years. But ultimately, the faction chose to take the risk and build an organization that better matched the radical collective identities they had forged with other local radical women's groups, especially GWL.

Conclusion

When factions develop at the chapter level, NOW's bureaucratic and federated structure creates a double-edged sword. NOW fosters a tremendous amount of creativity and diversity in its approaches to feminism by pulling in local activists of all stripes to create chapters that reflect local communities and sensibilities. And because of its flexibility at the chapter level, NOW's structure has proven durable over time, remaining the largest and longest-running feminist organization in the United States. But NOW members have sometimes had trouble bridging their local feminist identities and goals with NOW's national identity, which can feel distant and disconnected from their communities. Despite democratic representation on the national board of directors, rank-and-file members have often protested that national NOW priorities do not accurately reflect the work they want to be doing. As members grow disillusioned, local factions begin to think of national leaders as antagonists, hastening their exit from an organization that no longer feels like their own (Hirschman 1970).

While the dominant social movement perspective has been that nationally federated organizations like NOW are ideal for tamping down organizational conflict and retaining factions, it is precisely this federated structure that contributes to factionalism and eventual schism at the local level. The local factions I have detailed here developed out of a keenly felt mismatch between their local culture and priorities and what they perceived to be national NOW's agenda. This is a common problem in large, national, and federated organizations, in which local factions can rarely gather enough resources to genuinely challenge national leaders or create change in the broader organization (see Zald and Berger 1978). The Ohio NOW faction that eventually became WEAL recognized the futility of trying to outvote the East Coast chapters with their smaller Midwest chapters. In New York, The Feminists's faction tried to implement their organizational values in their local chapter before failing to change the mandated structures by national NOW. The Gainesville faction worked for many years and with several strategies to make changes to national NOW, including protesting at national conferences and staging events designed to pull national leaders into their agenda. Ultimately, none of the factions could pull national NOW in their direction, and each broke away to form new groups.

The cultural mismatch between local factions and national NOW operates as a push factor for these factions. But there are also pulls that factor in their choice to schism; each faction had developed a divergent ideology and identity in relationship with local, external connections. In other words, the factions found connections in their local communities that confirmed and often enhanced their disagreements with national NOW. Each of these factions experienced the local "boundary issues" that make large organizations more likely to experience schism (Liebman, Sutton, and Wuthnow 1988). The geographical dispersion of NOW members meant they had more in common with other local groups, with whom there was often significant membership overlap. These external connections, both when more conservative, as with Feminists for Life, and when more radical, as with the Gainesville NOW faction, shaped each faction's ideas about what feminism should be and provided models of activism outside of NOW's boundaries.

Scholars are less likely to notice this pattern of factionalism and schism, in part because it is happening at the local level and is inherently harder to track and enumerate than splits happening at the national level. The local level of social movements is often obscured by the activities, agendas, ideologies, and culture at the national organizational level (McCarthy 2005). The factions I detail here serve as an important reminder to pay attention to the skirmishes happening at the local level, where activists are embedded in particular cultures and networks, that are often a poor fit with national organizations, and that have the greatest motivation to schism.

Of course, factionalism doesn't just occur at the local level. In the next chapter, I examine what happens to factions that emerge at the core of the organization, on or around the board of directors. Just as the nationally federated structure limits the ability of peripheral factions to influence the national level, the same structure enables core factions to pursue their agenda in surprising ways rather than break away to form new groups. These divergent outcomes in the same organization offer evidence that structure does not provide the same opportunities to all members. Depending on their origins, some factions have greater voice than others, leaving others no alternative but to break away. In the next chapter, I turn to those with greater voice to examine how their factionalism plays out differently.

CHAPTER FOUR

Sticking at the Top

National Factionalism and the Choice to Stay

In 1975, a faction of NOW national board members calling themselves the Majority Caucus created and mailed a newsletter, *Electric Circle,* to NOW members explaining why they were better than their rival board faction Womansurge. They wrote, "The Majority Caucus members of the board favor a more democratic NOW with a strong national, strong states, and strong chapters. . . . It was out of this struggle that the Majority Caucus was first formed." They included specific instructions on how to support the Majority Caucus at the upcoming conference as well as detailed critiques of specific members of Womansurge. The newsletter closed with a manifesto, titled "Toward a Feminist Ethos," declaring that feminism is about cooperation, sacrifice, and sisterhood even among those who disagree (*Electric Circle* 1975, 5, 10).

Electric Circle was just one shot fired in a protracted battle in NOW between Womansurge and the Majority Caucus lasting through most of the 1970s. In the last chapter, I argued that NOW's structure provides an incubator for schism at the local level by allowing a high degree of differentiation while simultaneously frustrating their attempts to reform the national organization. In this chapter, I turn my attention to factions that emerged in NOW's core and investigate if and how groups battling at the top of the organization fare differently than those at the local level. National leaders argue over many of the same issues as local factions, especially when it comes to reconciling different priorities, tactics, and political strategies. Even though they occur in the same organizational structure and fight over the same issues, national factions are fighting in a different terrain than those originating in local chapters.

There are good theoretical reasons to believe that national factions might take different paths from their local counterparts. Dissatisfied members have limited choices: passively and loyally wait for their organization to change, actively voice their anger and try to force the organization to change, or leave (Hirschman 1970; Withey and Cooper 1989; Dowding et al. 2000). But these choices are not equally available to all members. At the organizational core, factions have access to opportunities and resources not available to peripheral factions. National-level factions, either on the board of directors or among national officers, have a greater ability to rally members across the nation to their side and to move their campaigns to new parts of the organization when they face road blocks. NOW's structure creates opportunities for the losers of national-level fights to stay in the organization—options that are much less plausible for the factions that originate in peripheral locations. With additional opportunities for mobilizing, national factions encounter less pressure to break away. At the same time, their position as national-level factions ties their collective identities more tightly to NOW's organizational identity, making it more difficult for them to imagine leaving NOW. In this way, a decentralized bureaucratic structure does help organizations prevent factionalism from becoming schisms, especially when those factions emerge in the organizational core.

National NOW

The national level of NOW was the most clearly and strategically planned part of the organization. At their first annual meeting in October 1966, thirty of NOW's charter members hammered out the details of the new organization with a statement of purpose that would guide the national agenda and a framework for organizational decision-making. It would be democratic, with members voting at annual conferences for bylaws and leaders. In between the conferences, a board of directors made up of thirty-five members and five national officers would act on behalf of the organization. The board would meet every three months, in rotating cities. Between these meetings, NOW officers would carry out the work agreed upon at the last board meeting. NOW founders were savvy political actors who understood the public media messaging needed to launch their organization. They swiftly built the organization's national brand, and for both its allies and its critics, NOW became the face of the emerging feminist movement.

NOW's early success was also a magic show, with founders encouraging the public illusion that NOW "was bigger and more powerful than it was" (Davis 1999, 57). For the first several years, its broader structure was makeshift, as leaders balanced growing and nurturing their young organization at the local level with the need to grasp a cultural moment suddenly sensitive to its claims. Hindsight is clear that they opted for an aggressive national agenda at the expense of developing a structure that worked for grassroots members. NOW headquarters rarely had anyone available to answer the phone or return mail from potential recruits (Freeman 1975), and its leaders neglected to provide a clear plan for establishing and incorporating chapters. The founding documents merely make note that chapter formation was possible where members desired it. For a number of early years, this left rank-and-file members to figure out organizational policy on their own (Barakso 2004).

In this loose arrangement, chapters were free from national control, and the board was free from the routine duties of representing specific constituents. On one hand, this allowed maximum freedom at the chapter level to create and experiment with forms that would resonate with their local communities. On the other hand, despite the leaders' expressed desire to have democratic control by members, board members exerted outsized control over the direction of the national organization. Small factions of leaders could influence the board of directors into support for controversial positions, including a call for the repeal of all abortion restrictions and support for the Equal Rights Amendment (ERA). The early disconnect between national NOW and local chapters drove much of NOW's early factionalism.

Recognizing the problem, NOW leaders debated over how to reform its structure in ways that would give chapters greater support and provide the board with more grounded authority to pursue a truly representative agenda. After a lengthy internal battle, leaders developed the bureaucratic tissue between local chapters and the national board. In 1970, the board restructured NOW along regional lines, including a West, Midwest, East, and South region, each with its own director who would coordinate the local chapters. But the change didn't resolve the worst of the communication problems, and by 1973, chapters in California and New York began threatening to withhold dues from national NOW until a state level of the organization was developed and national agreed to give back a greater portion of the membership dues to support it. By 1975, members voted to consider a delegate voting system rather than restricting voting only to those who could afford the time and money to travel to the national conference. Even as leaders worked to empower the grass roots of the organization, the board of directors remained the dominant force in determining the organization's national agenda (Barakso 2004; Gilmore 2013).

Because of its authority, the board of directors has been a frequent site of factionalism, and leaders organize periodically into competing camps. The board's power is lessened at the regional, state, and chapter levels of the organization, which have retained a great deal of freedom from board oversight. Grassroots members and local leaders can pick and choose which of the national priorities they focus on. They can also work on other projects, even those outside of NOW's official priorities, as long as they do not conflict with NOW's platforms. In effect, this means that after losing important battles at the national level, factions have many additional rungs of NOW's ladder from which they can continue their fight. This gives factions emerging at the top of the organization more flexibility to use the bureaucratic structure to their advantage than members at lower levels. Two groups, Womansurge and the Young Feminists, demonstrate how factionalism emerging at the top of the organization operates differently than conflicts emerging in the organization's peripheral locations, in terms of both opportunities and constraints on splitting from NOW.

The Rise of Womansurge

From the late 1960s to the early 1970s, NOW experienced significant growing pains as national leaders and local members struggled over how to reform the organization toward a more stable and democratic model. Local members resented the fact that their dues went to the national level when they received very little back in terms of support or communication from national leaders. Leading the charge for an additional state level, the California and New York chapters argued that the extra bureaucracy would improve both services and communication between the national and local levels. Members and leaders were also debating a shift in voting procedures. The original bylaws mandated that only members attending the annual conference could vote on organizational policy and leaders. The arrangement disadvantaged members who could not afford the time or money to attend the conference every year. Instead, reformers wanted a delegate system that would enable more NOW members to participate in organizational decision-making. The delegate option was initially introduced and rejected in 1972. Support continued to grow, however, for a change to voting procedures (Barakso 2004).

The NOW board of directors split on these issues, forming factions that represented different approaches for reforming the organization (Toni Carabillo and Judith Meuli Papers 1991; Carden 1975; National Organization for Women Records 1975c). The battles between the factions were particularly brutal between 1974 and 1976, as they competed in a series of tense board meetings and national elections. In 1974, members from Chicago ran for national office as a slate and campaigned for their platform at the conference—a new approach that was perceived as an aggressive and unwelcome change to conference procedures. Many of the women attending the conference had developed their feminist consciousness in the liberation wing of the movement, and the open politicking of the "Chicago Machine" violated their sense of sisterhood (Tully 1992; Freeman 1975). In response, a second faction of national leaders formed, arguing that NOW was growing too centralized and that reforms should include a redistribution of both power and resources to the local level. The split resulted in the election of a president, Karen DeCrow, from the latter faction and a board made up primarily of the former faction (Toni Carabillo and Judith Meuli Papers 1991; Staggenborg 1991). The main issues of contention between the two sides were how to bring about a delegate system of member voting, whether to endorse particular political candidates, and what it meant to bring women into "the mainstream" of American life.

The division between the two sides continued to widen when, in December 1974, a board meeting in New Orleans erupted over how to handle a dispute between President DeCrow and the executive director, Jane Plitt. The factions split on whom they supported, and the president's faction walked out of the meeting. In their absence, the remaining board members passed a series of controversial motions, including the decision to send NOW members a mail ballot for instituting the delegate system. When the walk-outs learned about the motions, they sued NOW and successfully convinced the judge that the ballot violated the organization's bylaws. The disastrous meeting and subsequent fallout crystalized the competing factions, with the president's faction naming itself the "Majority Caucus," in the belief that they represented the majority of members' preferences, and the other going by "Womansurge," named by member Betty Friedan for its dual message of Woman's Urge and Woman Surge (Tully 1992). Both factions "returned to their states and began organizing support for their position" among local chapters (Toni Carabillo and Judith Meuli Papers 1991).

By 1975, the rift between the rival factions had grown to the point that leaders feared the organization would break in half. In May, the

Majority Caucus held their own meeting for aligned members to settle on an agenda for the national conference, including a proposal for a constitutional convention to restructure NOW's bylaws. Womansurge members responded by calling an emergency meeting of the national board and mailing a statement in advance to board members, state coordinators, and chapter presidents announcing their intention to move the annual conference from Philadelphia to St. Louis. Their given reason was that St. Louis would offer a central location and better "represent the whole organization" (Toni Carabillo and Judith Meuli Papers 1991, 11). Their unwritten motivation was that many East Coast chapters, especially Philadelphia's, were aligned with the Majority Caucus, and Womansurge feared that a conference there would swamp their faction. Majority Caucus–aligned chapters declared that they would meet in Philadelphia even if the board voted to move the conference. Under the threat of two competing conferences and another bruising lawsuit, the Womansurge faction relented and the October conference moved forward as planned in Philadelphia.

After vigorous campaigns from both sides at the national conference, the Majority Caucus gained control of the board and retained control of the presidency. Rather than ending the fight, the Majority Caucus's successes exacerbated the factionalism. The Majority Caucus announced that NOW would embrace a more disruptive style of protest, including sit-ins and interfering with congressional hearings. Two of the victors, Karen DeCrow and Toni Carabillo, took public shots at Womansurge members, telling *Time* magazine, respectively, that Womansurge was a tiny splinter faction of aging professional women representing "a condescending view of what feminism is like" and that their "pattern of professional lobbying has slowed [NOW] down" (*Time* 1975). Womansurge members countered that the Majority Caucus was going to scare average women away. Betty Friedan told the *Time* reporter that the Majority Caucus had already caused many women to drop out of NOW because they no longer identified with its "sexual preoccupation and radical rhetoric." NOW's radical drift, she claimed, threatened to undo a decade of feminist progress. Womansurge also drafted a letter to NOW members directly, complaining that the Majority Caucus had begun blocking them from chairing the task forces or committees responsible for carrying out NOW's agenda (National Organization for Women Records 1976a). Frustrated by their loss of power in an organization they had considered their own, thirteen board members, including several NOW founders, met in New Orleans that November to discuss their options for forming an alternative organization (Tully 1992).

The evidence is murky on how seriously Womansurge considered the idea of breaking away. They certainly could have broken away—they had the skills and experience they would need to start over with a new organization, and its members were prominent enough to take an immediate leadership role in the feminist movement. According to Toni Carabillo's and Judith Meuli's (both members of the Majority Caucus) account of the split between NOW leaders, Womansurge's plan was to create a "politically astute leadership circle in every state/chapter" (Toni Carabillo and Judith Meuli Papers 1991, 12). But it is unclear whether this refers to a wholly new organization or if they meant that Womansurge would organize within existing NOW chapters. Womansurge member Wendy Winkler told *Time* magazine that they had no intention of becoming a rival membership organization to NOW, but she ended the interview with the threat, "If the leadership of NOW is so alienated from its members that there is no place to go, we may become a viable alternative to NOW."

Whatever initial interest they had in forming a new organization, the dissidents ultimately elected to remain in NOW. Shelley Fernandez (telephone interview with the author, March 1, 2010), former president of San Francisco NOW, explains that they decided not to leave for both ideological and strategic reasons:

> That takes a lot of money, energy, time. . . . We already had a NOW organization. Betty Friedan [Womansurge member] started it. Why should we break away from it? We just have to make our presence known within it. You know, it's better to work within to make changes.

Fernandez's sentiments were echoed by Mary Jean Tully (1992), who was serving as the head of NOW's Legal Defense and Education Fund at the time Womansurge was organizing. She recalled a complicated mix of collective identity ties and organizational fatigue in the decision to stay a part of NOW rather than break away:

> How many organizations can you be in on in the founding of? Even though most of us had not been in on the founding, we had still been in on the early days, so we just didn't have what it took to do it.

Womansurge members' roles as national leaders worked to keep them in the organization in several ways. Their role in creating and shaping NOW in its early years provided them with a sense of ownership—and a collective identity tied to that ownership—that made breaking away less appealing. And because they were working from the top of the organization, they also had access to resources that made breaking away less necessary than for factions emerging in NOW's periphery.

For example, even after losing board seats in mid-1970s elections and being blocked from important committee assignments, many Womansurge members still leveraged their membership on the board to continue their fight. They used the national board meetings, happening four times a year, as a forum for their own faction's meetings. They would meet immediately before the official board assembled to set their goals and establish how they would vote in the board meeting. This strategy allowed the geographically dispersed faction to regularly come together and confirm their agenda as a united faction.

Womansurge members also used their position at the top of NOW's federated structure, pushing for their priorities among local members. They actively campaigned across the entire organization, lobbying individual chapters and states to support their priorities at the national conferences. In a 1975 letter explaining their vision for NOW's future, Womansurge members wrote,

> Please contact us if you would like someone to visit your NOW group to provide trainings and/or to provide further explanation of the events in the organization, and how we can work together to build an organization that can effect real changes for all women. (Maren Lockwood Carden Papers 1975)

By courting local and state chapters, Womansurge members consciously used their national profiles to raise allies in NOW's periphery. Fernandez confirmed the strategy, highlighting how NOW's federated design helped her faction build a broader foundation of support:

> Those of us in Womansurge who worked within NOW did go to many meetings across the country—state meetings and local meetings—and talked about our priorities. So yeah, sure we got space [at the local level], but we were NOW national board members, and all of the states, they all wanted to talk to national board members.

NOW's general commitment to democracy meant that support from local and state chapters could eventually swing NOW's national agenda back toward Womansurge's preferences. But this required a campaign strategy oriented toward the grass roots of the organization, building support through direct contact with as many chapters as possible. Womansurge members had the financial capacity to travel for their board of director responsibilities, and they were capable of doing the same on behalf of their narrower faction within NOW leadership.

Structural opportunities for the Womansurge faction were evident in other ways as well. When the Majority Caucus blocked them from implementing their priorities on the national level, many Womansurge members shifted the focus of their work back to their home state and local chapters. Womansurge member Judith Lonnquist, for example, lost her seat on the board, but rather than accept defeat, she ran for and was elected president of NOW's Seattle chapter. In an interview with the Washington Women's History Consortium, Lonnquist remembers this as a period of continued conflict between the ascending Majority Caucus faction and the seemingly vanquished Womansurge members: "I had plenty of other feminist work for me and plenty of other avenues to accomplish change. So I came back to Seattle and was elected chapter president, just so I could be a thorn in Ellie's [Majority Caucus leader and NOW president] side" (Lonnquist 2007). For Lonnquist and other Womansurge members, moving to leadership positions in the lower levels of the organization provided a way to continue their fight against the Majority Caucus. These options did not provide a resolution to the conflict, or even necessarily concrete victories for Womansurge, but they did offer a way for Womansurge to avoid breaking away from NOW.

While NOW struggled with factionalism through much of the 1970s, by the end of 1976, the worst of the crisis had passed. At the 1976 conference, the membership agreed on proposals to institute a delegate voting system and the election of national board members from the regions rather than at the national conference. Eleanor Smeal became NOW president in 1977, and she focused the organization's attention on ratifying the ERA. No issue helped to blend the factions more than this common fight (M. J. Collins, telephone interview with the author, May 29, 2009). The ERA became NOW's top priority, and it devoted the bulk of its organizational resources to fighting for its passage. Over time, new board members were elected who were not affiliated with either faction. The issues that had initially divided the organization blurred together, and both factions faded away. A generation after the tense battle between Womansurge and the Majority Caucus, another fight began brewing at the national level of NOW, revolving around young women and their lack of representation on the board of directors.

Rise of the Young Feminists

Liberal second-wave organizations have long been criticized for focusing on the interests of older women at the expense of younger women's priorities. Young feminists have frequently organized within NOW in efforts to make older, professional leaders recognize their distinct perspectives and needs. Beginning as early as the 1970s, members pressed NOW leaders for an expanded vision of feminist activism that included many of the theories and styles developed in the younger liberation wing of the movement. For example, young members wanted NOW to incorporate "rap groups" into local chapters. Otherwise called consciousness-raising circles, these groups were designed to educate recent converts on the relevance of feminism to their personal lives. Older NOW leaders were reluctant to incorporate consciousness-raising groups because they wanted to maintain the organization's image as "action oriented." They argued that internally focused consciousness raising might sap the energy needed for externally directed activism. Under pressure from younger members, local chapters began regularly holding rap groups, and older members soon saw their value as a way to quickly orient new members and build feminist solidarity. Many chapters made consciousness-raising groups a permanent part of their structure—New York City NOW created a consciousness-raising subcommittee, other chapters put together consciousness-raising courses for new members, and Los Angeles NOW published its own consciousness-raising handbook in 1974. Young women had effectively changed the way many local NOW chapters worked by incorporating the activism styles and preferences of the liberation branch of the movement (Freeman 1975).

At the national level, younger NOW members have traditionally had a much harder time making their voices heard, even when leaders are actively courting their support. Beginning in the late 1980s and throughout the 1990s, NOW passed a series of conference resolutions designed to incorporate young women into national leadership. In 1988, NOW resolved to start a Campus Mobilization Campaign to recruit and train young women from college campuses. NOW leaders saw this as a promising way to incorporate young leaders into the NOW national structure. In 1991, NOW members declared that the "younger heirs of the feminist movement," in coordination with national NOW, would organize a "week of local direct action," with an undefined "major nationally coordinated action as its centerpiece." In that same year, national NOW hosted its first Young Feminists conference, which focused on issues like sexual assault and reproductive rights. The event was organized mostly by older NOW leaders and reflected their sense of what young feminists needed (Whittier 2006). At that conference, young members passed their own resolution calling for NOW to establish a Young Feminist Conference

Implementation Committee (CIC)—a standing committee that would review "all current and future NOW policies from the perspective of young feminists." In 1993, NOW vowed to recruit and nurture young women's leadership in a variety of ways, including holding a Young Feminist Issues hearing at every future NOW national conference and hosting a second conference exclusively for young feminists. The organization also promised to add at least one staff position at the NOW Action Center devoted specifically to young feminist issues and organizing. In 1994, the Young Feminist CIC was charged with organizing a national Summit on Violence that would focus on young women's vulnerability to violence. In 1995, NOW members voted to devote greater space in the *National NOW Times* to young feminists and their issues as well as to "actively seek out a young feminist membership and encourage young members to run for NOW leadership at local, state, and national levels." The very next year, NOW held a conference focused on young feminists and vowed to create mentoring programs to nurture them as well as to make "young feminist issues" a higher priority by adding workshops and networking opportunities for younger members. In 1997, NOW held a Young Feminist Summit devoted to developing young women's leadership in the organization and in their local communities. Members voted again and again to pay special attention to young feminists and to promote their interests (National Organization for Women, n.d.-d, n.d.-e). Yet, for these resolutions, committees, and conferences, little seemed to change in the organization, and many young women remained disillusioned about their ability to affect NOW's agenda.

Young members' frustration erupted at the national conference in 2003. Rebecca Walker, an activist devoted to boosting young women's distinct feminist perspective, accepted NOW's Intrepid Award—an honor given by NOW and the NOW foundation to recognizing "resolutely courageous, fearless and bold women" (National Organization for Women, n.d.-f). In her acceptance speech, Walker was openly critical of NOW leadership on many issues, including their failure to prioritize young women's perspectives (Barakso 2004). Perhaps galvanized by Walker's address, a faction of young members proposed a bylaw change that would require national NOW to make a permanent seat on the board of directors dedicated to a member under thirty years old. While there had regularly been women under thirty years old on the board throughout NOW's history, the new bylaws represented a way to routinize young women's influence at the national level. Older members did not share their enthusiasm for changing the bylaws, and it quickly became clear that the resolution was not going to find enough support on the floor of the conference.

The faction sought advice from Eleanor Smeal, who had moved from the NOW presidency to form the Feminist Majority Foundation. With Smeal's help, the Young Feminists arranged a compromise—rather than a permanent seat on the board, NOW leaders agreed to develop a national advisory task force for feminists aged thirty or under. The task force would provide suggestions for the board on issues significant to younger women. The faction agreed to the compromise and was institutionalized in the form of a nonbinding advisor to the board on "matters of agenda, leadership, recruitment and issue prioritization regarding young feminists in NOW" (National Organization for Women, n.d.-c). The Young Feminists Task Force (YFTF) includes roughly a dozen members each year who are appointed to serve by the president after they have been nominated by other members in the organization. The task force tends to focus on issues of body image, violence, mentoring, and other health concerns common for younger women. Like other advisory task forces in NOW, the YFTF has no voting power on the board of directors.

Much like Womansurge a generation before, the Young Feminists had a presence in NOW's core but also found themselves isolated from actual influence or power in determining NOW's future. Despite the energy coming from the YFTF and its ambitious agenda, its location relative to the board slowed their momentum. The central problem was organizational; new members cycled on each year, meaning the task force was constantly starting anew. According to the first chair of the task force, Erin Matson (telephone interview with the author, May 18, 2009), the group essentially "had the same meeting every year" because few of the new members had organizational skills or experience in setting priorities and carrying out an achievable agenda. This structure was mandated in the bylaws, giving the Young Feminists little freedom to alter it in ways that would give them more independence.

Moreover, because the task force had been a quick compromise to quell factionalism among the young members, neither the NOW leaders nor the Young Feminists had developed a clear plan for how the task force would fit with the routine business of the board. This was a chronic point of frustration for task force members, who struggled to get board members to take their recommendations seriously. One clear example of this struggle is the Young Feminists' fight, starting in 2006, to get NOW to campaign for expanded access to the human papillomavirus (HPV) vaccine.

HPV is an extremely common sexually transmitted disease that disproportionately affects younger women and causes most cervical cancer cases. When a vaccine was developed to prevent strains of HPV known to cause cancer, the Young Feminists lobbied the board to launch a national campaign for women's access to the vaccine. Ultimately, the board of directors chose not to prioritize the campaign out of concern that the vaccine was an attempt by large pharmaceutical companies to make money from women's bodies. Already frustrated about its lack of influence on the board of directors, this disagreement further deteriorated the Young Feminists' relationship with NOW's board of directors. They faced a choice about continuing in NOW or pursuing their interests with a new organization. Like Womansurge, the YFTF activists chose to stay by taking their fight to a different part of the organization.

Matson explained their strategy to make the vaccine a priority, despite the refusal of the board:

> I, being one of the people who felt very strongly about it, decided with my state board to take it up locally. So we had a grassroots action campaign in the state but it did not go anywhere nationally. There was talk [on the YFTF] of "I'm going to work on this locally" and "I'm going to work on this locally, too," because that way we could skirt—we could work on what we wanted without having to wait for someone else to do something about. It circumvents the lack of a national [campaign].

Matson acknowledges that she and her fellow task force members actively sought a way around the decision of the national board not to pursue the vaccine campaign. This strategy was made possible because of the bureaucratic and federated structure of NOW, which provided enormous space and freedom in its peripheral locations. Matson explains the structure this way:

> Local chapters are free to pursue whatever they want as long as it doesn't conflict with NOW policy, and given that there was not policy about [the HPV vaccine], it was ripe for the picking. . . . It was simply that this was the issue people wanted to work on and they did it where they could.

In effect, the young feminist faction was able to continue their fight within NOW by using the federated structure, with its freedom at the peripheral levels, to evade negative decisions of the board.

While both the Young Feminists and Womansurge were able to capitalize on their national presence and NOW's hierarchy to continue their fights inside of NOW, the Young Feminists were handicapped in a way that Womansurge was not. When the Young Feminists accepted the offer to be formalized as an advisory task force, the faction agreed to play by the rules established by the board of directors. The original faction of young members was broken up into those who went through this process and those who did not. As a result, many of the women who were initially the most passionate about the issues left the task force for good, or never joined it in the first place. Some of the early members moved into the established routes to power in NOW. Matson, for example, became a member of the board of directors through her position as a regional director. She also encouraged other young members of the task force to make similar moves rather than spending their time on the advisory council. In 2009, she became the national action vice president of NOW. Other young members left NOW completely, after years of feeling "like they were hitting up against a brick wall."

Institutionalizing the Young Feminists as a task force has also had ambiguous effects on NOW's policy. Many issues that young women championed, particularly reproductive rights and violence issues, continued to receive attention and resources from national NOW. But there was already deep consensus among NOW members that these issues were important. On more divisive issues, like the HPV vaccine, the YFTF does not seem to have been able to sway the board to their perspective in any substantial way. And while there was a flurry of resolutions framed around the interests of young feminists between 1988 and the mid-2000s, more recent conference resolutions barely mention young feminists at all. Of the resolutions listed on NOW's website between 2008 and 2014, not a single one mentions young feminists or their unique perspectives as an organizational priority. The YFTF continues to hold sessions and workshops at the national conference but NOW has not held a conference specifically for young women since 2006.

Conclusion

Comparing the cases of local schism to the national factions discussed here, we can see a deeper story about how organizational structure and factional location work in tandem to constrain or enable schism. Emerging at the national level, Womansurge and the Young Feminists were able to capitalize on all of the advantages of NOW's federated and bureaucratic structure. Even after losing important battles, their access to the national board was a consistent opportunity and source of hope for affecting national NOW's priorities. Because the board meets regularly, the factions could press for their agenda and lobby others on the board multiple times a year. Most importantly, even when they failed to sway other national board members, their association with national NOW gave them privileges at other levels of the organization. Both Womansurge and the Young Feminists were able to move their activism to lower levels of the organization, where they faced less resistance. Womansurge members took their campaign a step further by traveling from chapter to chapter directly promoting their view to rank-and-file NOW members.

In this way, the freedom members enjoy in NOW's peripheral spaces works in distinct ways depending on where the factions emerge. Factions originating in chapters are free to orient their activism however they wanted. But their dissent was often directed up the hierarchy to national leaders who seem disconnected and out of touch with rank-and-file concerns. But chapter factions had no national forum to help spread their vision for the organization to other NOW members, so their grievances remained concentrated in the local areas where they initiated. When they ran into a wall of resistance, they had nowhere else to take their agenda, except out of NOW in the form of schisms. In contrast, national NOW factions were better able to capitalize on the freedom granted to local chapters in the bureaucratic system. Their national status and geographic dispersion helped to spread their ideas and build a wider base of support across NOW. And they had a greater ability to implement their priorities at the regional and state levels, when blocked or ignored by the national board of directors.

Of course, another way of interpreting the distinct trajectories of national and local factions is that national factions were more constrained than local factions in breaking away. One of the key steps in forming a breakaway organization is that the faction has developed a strong collective identity (Dyck and Starke 1999). When they form at local levels, factions likely enjoy tighter identity bonds than those that form at the national level. Local faction members live near each other, enabling them to meet frequently. They know each other well, and they share a community outside of and beyond NOW. This likely helps them envision new relationships with each other that are not conditioned on their membership in NOW.

In contrast to the strong, localized collective identities of the chapter factions, the national factions' collective identities are built through their work in NOW. Womansurge's collective identity was based in members' common experience as NOW founders and early leaders, and this could not be easily transferred to a new organization. And evidence is scant for how well developed the young feminist collective identity was to begin with. The faction's quick decision to accept the task force compromise meant it had little time to build a distinct identity that could survive independently of NOW. Both factions were also geographically dispersed around the country. They could meet at most a few times a year in person, and each meeting was arranged around official national NOW business. They may have agreed as factions to implement their common agendas at lower levels of NOW, but each member carried out this work individually. For both national factions, they had few other opportunities to build a collective identity that could grow outside of NOW's boundaries, making breaking away from NOW both less appealing and less viable. In this way, NOW's organizational structure enables national factions to continue their fights in NOW over long periods of time, at the same time as it constrains their options to break away.

In the next chapter, I turn to the peripheral task force structure as a site of immense creativity and generation for both NOW and the broader feminist movement. Task forces are structured with a particular mix of structural freedom and constraints, making them ripe places for factionalism and splitting.

CHAPTER FIVE

Fracturing Task Forces

In July 1973, a small group of leaders reported to the NOW board of directors a list of fundamental challenges facing the organization's task forces, the committees designated to carry out NOW's mission. The group, representing the newly created Task Force on Task Forces, identified three key problems: task forces were disconnected from the board of directors, they were underfunded, and they lacked information about what resources were available to them as a part of NOW's structure. Task force members felt marginalized and undervalued by NOW's board of directors, hindering their efforts to combat gender inequality in the broader society. The report highlighted the leaders' growing alarm about their lack of resources and the difficult choices required of them because of it. "A financial crisis for the Task Forces," they argued, "is a program crisis for the organization" (National Organization for Women Records 1973a, 2).

NOW's paper archive from the 1970s provides a glimpse into the organizational dilemma created by the task force structure at a particularly fraught time in the organization. The task forces were a home for members who cared about specific, even idiosyncratic issues, uniting them with members across the country who cared as much as they did and who they would not have found without NOW to unite them. Task forces were relatively small groups of NOW members who cared about their particular issues in a way other members and leaders did not, especially in the years dominated by the Equal Rights Amendment (ERA) and NOW's growing emphasis on protecting reproductive rights. Isolated and underfunded, these groups were often frustrated by the inherent limitations of being in the periphery of a bureaucratic structure. Despite the problems in this part of the organization, the list of task forces and committees continued to grow during this time period. NOW created dozens of new task forces, even as existing ones were starved of organizational resources to do their work.

Of course, this was not what NOW founders had intended when they created its bureaucratic structure—when they viewed the task forces as the main engine for achieving their vision of social change. In the late 1960s, feminists confronted a world in which sexism was built into every social, political, and cultural institution. Surveying this landscape, NOW founders constructed an organization that would maximize freedom for members to address whatever issues they wanted with only a minimal level of coordination at the national level. Initially, NOW intended to focus on seven "targets for action": employment equality, educational opportunities, social equality, media portrayals of women, poverty, equal rights, and religious institutions. These were drawn from the founders' own interests and what they expected would make the biggest difference in women's lives. The task forces were designed to draw on the talents and knowledge of specialists who would carry out the "necessary strategic planning and research on a national basis and to assist the chapters in being able to work together on a coordinated program" (National Organization for Women Records 1973a).

New members across the country flocked to NOW, energized and anxious to tackle inequality, demanding a wider and more aggressive agenda. Mary Jean Collins (telephone interview with the author, May 29, 2009), an early member of NOW's board of directors and its task force coordinator in the 1970s, recounts the explosion of areas on which members wanted to work:

> These task forces [were formed] on every topic you can think of and they kept evolving. So it was women and employment, women and the arts, women in religion, women in business, women and the issue of rape, the issue of domestic violence, displaced homemakers, volunteerism. On it went.

As the organization grew, new leaders and members brought additional ideas for what the organization could address. The task forces did the groundwork in pursuing NOW's agenda to eliminate sexism from political, economic, and cultural institutions. At the chapter level, members often created their own campaigns to address the issues that were meaningful to them and their communities (see chapter 3). Often, these local campaigns overlapped with national-level priorities, and chapters frequently asked for more support and resources from the national level in the form of a task force devoted to the issue. The number of NOW task forces ballooned to include a broad swath of new issues and identities.

By the late 1970s, leaders began employing different organizational schemes to manage NOW's ever-expanding agenda without limiting the actual number of issues. They tried combining them into a smaller number and then creating superstructures that would coordinate multiple task forces at once without reducing the total number. NOW renamed and reorganized the dozens of issues its members wanted to address into task forces, committees, conference implementation committees, ad hoc committees, advisory committees, issue consultant committees, and standing committees (National Organization for Women, n.d.-a). The dizzying array of shifting bureaucratic arrangements symbolized the deeper, inherent challenge these kinds of organizations face as they try to carry a broad agenda with limited time, energy, and financial resources. The archival record makes it clear that these efforts were generally met with frustrated task force members threatening to break away. Some followed through, creating independent specialized organizations, even if still friendly and collaborative with the organization they had left behind.

For all this trouble, it is also clear why NOW adopted the task force structure. Including a high number of issues allows the organization to reach a wide diversity potential members, seek resources from multiple pools, and hedge against losses in any one arena. These features make groups like NOW large, stable, and durable. Yet, over the organization's history, the issues were divided across the organization's core and periphery in ways that seeded factionalism and schism. Members who cared about peripheralized issues frequently grew frustrated by the constant haggling with the national board of directors for meager resources. Unhappy with their secondary status, clusters of task force members sometimes reinvented their groups outside of NOW and apart from its issue pecking order.

These clusters of members knew that breaking away would come at a high cost. NOW's name and reputation carried a great deal of weight in the feminist movement and with the broader public. But breaking away would also remove the burden of that reputation in other contexts. As an independent group, they might benefit from a lower profile and enjoy easier working relationships with institutions and elites who had been skeptical of NOW's boisterous protest reputation (Kretschmer 2014). Independence from NOW would also bring economic freedom, if also greater economic risk. After breaking away, money raised would all be kept for the issues and projects they cared about, rather than being routed through a national board. Having first come together as one small committee of a large, formalized, general organization, task force members often struggled over the benefits and costs of this organizational arrangement. Many decided that the risks of starting over independently were worth it. This chapter is devoted to outlining the schism process in these peripheralized task forces.

The Benefits and Costs of Tackling Everything in One Organization

In many circumstances, generalist groups have important advantages over specialized organizations. Groups need resources, like money and labor, to survive, and the more issues with which they engage, the wider is their base for recruiting support. Generalists are also better able to manage uncertainty in their environments. By embracing a broad range of issues, tactics, and constituencies, generalists disperse their risk and avoid the crippling effects of leaning too heavily on an issue waning in significance or on a declining resource base.

NOW is a testament to the scholarly optimism about the generalist form. Since its founding, NOW has had its hand in nearly every avenue of feminist activism, from national electoral politics and lobbying campaigns to grassroots consciousness-raising groups. Its early prominence in the movement and its work on so many issues mean that it is prominent in the cultural conversations about a wide array of feminist concerns. In describing her decision to work for NOW in the mid-1980s, Loretta Ross (2004) remembers the particular allure of NOW's status as the authority on all issues relating to women:

> One of the things that makes NOW stand out from the crowd . . . is that they are seen as "The Authority" on women's issues. So, when Reagan's supporting Sandra Day O'Connor for the Supreme Court, NOW doesn't have to send out a press release: CNN is on their doorsteps. And when the Challenger blew up, they came and asked us about what we felt about the schoolteacher, Christa McAuliffe, dying on the Challenger. . . . When you're seen as "The Authority" versus you're the wannabes, and that is the peculiar position NOW has enjoyed. . . . You find that a lot of their coalitional partners are trying to get NOW's press or trying to get that kind of credibility that NOW has on women's issues pretty effortlessly—I don't want to say effortlessly, but pretty naturally, as the first feminist organization.

Beyond its authority to garner media attention, NOW's expansive reach meant that its leaders could shift to new issues that were a better fit for shifting political conditions without needing to start from scratch each time. For example, in the 1970s, NOW leaders took a significant risk when they decided to go all in for the ERA, a single issue that sucked up much of the organization's energy and resources. It is hard to overestimate how large a hit national NOW took following the ERA loss, shedding both discouraged members and money. Yet it survived by reenergizing the other issues that had been put on the back burner for the better part of a decade. Its broad reach allowed NOW to attract members with diverse networks of contacts, interests, and talents that could be called up following the ERA defeat. With freedom at the local level, members continued to focus on the many issues NOW leaders had neglected, and the organization was able to pivot to these other areas. In this way, generalist organizations are better able to smooth out membership dips and dissents, and they have the infrastructure in place to withstand periods of withering economic, political, and cultural conditions.

While its generalist structure made NOW stable and durable, it also created the conditions under which internal groups of members felt isolated and underserved by those advantages. For many years, the only criterion for an issue being included in NOW's formal agenda was that a NOW member be willing to volunteer to head its task force. Sometimes these task forces were initiated by rank-and-file members at national conferences. At other times, a single interested member would petition the board of directors for a task force. New issues could be added easily to the already long list of issues NOW included. This was especially true given that the investment from NOW's administration was often very limited—sometimes only a few hundred dollars per task force per year. In this formulation, there were very few brakes to slow NOW's bureaucratic expansion.

As NOW adopted more and more issues, leaders struggled to balance the onslaught of demands generated by the new task forces and committees with the realities of priority setting. Task force coordinators were continually dismayed by how little funding they had to do their work, how little information was provided by the overworked board of directors, and how little autonomy they had to make decisions on their own. As the number of task forces grew, these problems only got worse.

From the 1970s through the 1990s, NOW leaders continuously tried to rein in the unwieldly task force branch of its organization. At times, leaders would suggest consolidating the task forces by creating new umbrella committees that would oversee several task forces at once. At other times, leaders would try to compel the diverse task forces to focus their energies in the same direction. The organizational record and activist interviews clarify the common struggles task forces faced as part of the generalist structure as well as the pressure they felt to strike out on their own.

Priority Setting and Funding Disputes

The broad reach of the organization meant few issues received consistent attention from the board of directors, or from any significant portion of the rest of the organization. From the outset, NOW leaders were ambitious and anxious to make tangible gains for women's equality. In this early rush, they took on much more than any one group could do. Starting with just seven priority issues, by 1974, the number of task forces had ballooned to thirty-five, including task forces on the arts; discrimination in the AT&T corporation; discrimination in Sears, Roebuck and Company; child care; compliance with discrimination laws; women's access to credit; education equality; the Federal Communications Commission; women's health; images of women in the media; labor issues; legal issues; legislative issues; marriage, divorce, and family concerns; the "masculine mystique"; minority women; nurses in NOW; politics; poverty; women in prison; older women; rape; religion; reproductive rights; sexuality; speakers bureaus; sports; stockholder actions; women's studies; taxes; and volunteerism (National Organization for Women Records 1974a). The archival record is clear that NOW leaders were open to a wide range of new task force proposals.

   The task force for nurses offers an instructive example of how task forces were formed and the problems that arose. In her report to the board in 1974, Mary Jean Collins requested that the board approve a permanent nurses' task force. She justified the request by noting:

> There is precedent in other constituency task forces in the [NOW]. . . . They have grown rapidly and there is widespread interest. They feel that with national status and access to NOW's PR resources they could more easily grow geographically. They plan to go to the American Nurses Association later this year and organize there. Their goals are feminist and they see feminism as adding significantly to the perspective and strength of organized nurses. They show the ability to develop [a] good program and attract new members and revenues to NOW. (National Organization for Women Records 1974b)

On the basis of Collins's recommendation, the board approved the proposal and made the task force an official part of NOW. In her first report to the board, Kathleen McInerney, the nursing task force coordinator, reported that she fielded fifty letters and twenty-five to thirty phone calls a week from people interested in NOW's work on nursing (National Organization for Women Records 1975f). Despite the promise of widespread interest from both NOW members and nurses across the nation, by 1975, the task force had only thirteen members (National Organization for Women Records 1975d). By comparison, of the thirty task forces listed that year, nursing had the second lowest count of members, surpassing only the Research Committee, with just six members. The average number of members for all task forces was eighty-four, a number pulled up dramatically by the Legislation and Compliance task forces, with 217 and 446 members, respectively. These task forces generated much more interest from members and leaders alike, leaving the less popular task forces to languish with low numbers and little financial support. After 1975, I found no more mention of the nursing task force in NOW's reports.

Most of the task forces suffered from benign neglect from the national board. They were carried by the passions of a handful of NOW members, or sometimes a single member, who was deeply knowledgeable about the specific issue and devoted to its importance. Ironically, in the same report proposing that the nurses' task force be formed and funded, Collins outlined the problem of this approach. National priorities, she argued, should drive funding decisions for task forces rather than blanket approval and funding for each new issue:

> With or without the budget crisis we do not have adequate money to fund all task forces at their requested levels. Rather than reducing all task forces to a flat grant level, I recommend setting priorities which are eligible for more funds than other task forces. These priorities would allow NOW to focus public attention on major efforts and successes; they could be the focus for membership drives, as in the abortion mailing done this spring. (National Organization for Women Records 1974b)

NOW's generalist orientation and swelling number of individual task forces also created problems as their coordinators struggled over how much they should be working together. The task force coordinators met in May 1974 to discuss the problems. In the resulting report, they noted:

We desperately need much more interaction among ourselves than is currently available. We emphatically believe that the substantive issues that face us regarding social change [are] all-[e]ncompassing and independent enough to require attention and cooperation from all of us. . . . We have high need to evolve a workable evaluation process regarding ourselves and our structure in order to determine our effectiveness and thence accountability to the membership. (National Organization for Women Records 1974f)

Task force coordinators begged the board for more control of their administration, asking for greater "responsibility for our own role and function within the organization and directly demonstrat[e] our accountability to the membership" (National Organization for Women Records 1974f).

Although the problem was plain, the solution was not. NOW's decentralized orientation made leaders reluctant to limit the organization to some predetermined set of issues. In an effort to manage the issue proliferation while maintaining all of the existing task forces, NOW leaders tried a variety of different bureaucratic solutions. Responding to a chapter president in 1974, President Wilma Scott Heide reported on the challenge of meeting all of the organization's conflicting demands: "There are several proposals around vis-à-vis task force areas, including combining 26 T.F. to 10 major areas. New interest groups seem to arise almost weekly and want to be national task forces" (National Organization for Women Records 1974c).

The "task forces team," made up of task force coordinators and a few board members, agreed that restructuring was necessary: there were too many task forces and "not enough coordination among existing ones" (National Organization for Women Records 1974e). They advocated for a middle ground of encouraging the current task forces to consolidate, or at least to collaborate in areas of common interest, including routine tasks like producing newsletters. Their report to the board, however, also makes it clear that, whatever the bureaucratic solution the task forces settled on, the task forces team wanted to continue to expand in new directions: "we strongly recommend the objective of keeping the total number of task forces constant—or less than the current number—while at the same time addressing new areas" (National Organization for Women Records 1974e).

In November 1975, President Karen DeCrow announced that she would be working with the board to reorganize the task forces, so that their work would be less "haphazard" (National Organization for Women Records 1975c). But this was followed just two months later by another letter from DeCrow, in which she asserted that the number of task forces would remain unchanged. She makes the organization's dilemma clear:

> We do not want to scatter our energies too widely; nevertheless we do want to encourage NOW members to work on all feminist issues of interest to them. To reduce the number of our task forces would be to deprive many chapters and states of valuable help in many areas and perhaps arbitrarily limit the number of issues on which NOW members and chapters can work. (National Organization for Women Records 1976b)

Stuck between the problems of limiting members' freedom and being too scattered, DeCrow and the board of directors tried to compromise. The number of task forces would stay the same, or even increase, if members came to leaders with new issues to address, but there should be greater coordination between the task forces. Most importantly, the task force coordinators were asked to focus on a set of core issues on which they would all work, regardless of their specific task force. In her letter announcing her decision to the national board, DeCrow wrote that, no matter what their issue area, task forces should emphasize the ERA ratification drive:

> Because the ERA is of such high priority for us, each task force ought to attempt to relate their particular substantive area to the ERA. . . . Each task force ought to publicize how the area of its particular concern will suffer if the ERA is not ratified, and how it will benefit with ratification. (National Organization for Women Records 1976a)

These directives did little to ease the frustrations of task force members, who did not receive an increase in funding or autonomy in the scheme. And it reinforced the hierarchy of priorities within NOW that had pressed many task forces into the periphery. Collins, serving as task force coordinator, generally supported the prioritization of some issues over others, having acknowledged that "certain task forces, by virtue of special funding [were] already in a different category," including legislation and the ERA, administrative committees, and reproductive rights (National Organization for Women Records 1974b). These areas were earmarked for greater funding from the NOW board or, as was the case with reproductive rights, benefited from special fund-raising efforts by national NOW. The rest of the areas were left to compete with each other, receiving resources based on "membership decisions, chapter interest, and changing circumstances to be evaluated from time to time in board priority votes and on an interim basis by our President in consultation with the task force coordinator" (National Organization for Women Records 1974b). In an undated memo from the same period, the Task Force Committee circulated suggestions for the process of deciding whether a task force should be maintained. It posed questions that NOW leaders should ask about each task force, including whether the issue sufficiently related to "our" goals and if there were "any other organizations better equipped to handle the purposes of this taskforce or already doing a very adequate job? . . . We should place primary emphasis and energy on those projects that will do the most for the greatest number of women in our society" (National Organization for Women Records, n.d.-a). The guidelines also noted that "with the size of this organization there should be at least fifteen or twenty chapters throughout the country interested in the subject." Given the small number of members on many of the task forces, it is unlikely that many reached that threshold.

If consolidation and collaboration were supposed to solve the problem of too many task forces, they also led to turf wars between them. Some members wanted a task force on sports, while others argued that it should instead be a special committee under the Education Task Force. There was a special ERA task force with only fifteen members, despite how important the ERA was in NOW generally. Instead, most of the ERA work was being done by the Legislation Task Force. The Coordination Committee (essentially another task force on the task forces) argued that ERA work should be consolidated under Legislation, while another Legislation subgroup, the Credit and Finance Committee, should be made into its own task force (National Organization for Women Records, n.d.-b). The bureaucratic wrangling continued into the late 1970s, when the NOW Executive Committee recommended to the board in summer 1977 that specific issues be reorganized around four central committees: the ERA Committee, the Human Rights Committee, the Societal Equality Committee, and the Economic Rights Committee (National Organization for Women Records 1977c).[1] As part of this reorganization, NOW brought its committees under tighter control of the national board by making them

---

1 The ERA Committee would tackle economic planning, women, and poverty; employment discrimination; full employment/minimum income; Social Security/pension plan discrimination; credit discrimination; pregnancy discrimination; and displaced homemakers committees. The Human Rights Committee would handle reproductive rights, rape and domestic violence, health care, and mental health. The Societal Equality Committee would focus on issues of media reform, lesbian rights, minority women, ageism and women, religious equality, early childhood development, education discrimination, marriage, and divorce.

standing "board committees." The structure continued to evolve through the 1980s and 1990s, as the oversight structure changed, names of committees changed, and new committees were regularly added, disbanded, or merged.

Each new organizational scheme resulted in the demotion of some issue committees. In a 1977 board report, despite representing several issues (formerly task forces), the Human Rights Committee had decided to "concentrate on reproductive rights and, therefore, all committee members will share information, decisions, and liaison of this issue." Whatever they were initially focused on, each committee should now "address reproductive rights issues immediately, particularly, the issue of abortion." The report carrying this change also requested that the board consider hiring a "full time staff person for reproductive rights" since the budget for that issue was already "somewhat large" and would need someone to "coordinate, facilitate, provide support and follow up for the reproductive rights program" (National Organization for Women Records 1977a). By 1979, the Human Rights Committee allotted $16,000 to its reproductive rights program but only about $1,000 to each of its four other issue areas (National Organization for Women Records 1979d).

Even in periods when the organization was not struggling for money, NOW resources were generally earmarked for specific projects, leaving most issues underfunded. This was especially true for the ERA fight, when the organization experienced explosive growth because of its leadership in the campaign (Kretschmer and Mansbridge 2017). Encouraged by the NOW board, many of the task forces devoted themselves to the ERA and neglected the other issues under their purview. In 1978, the Societal Equality Committee sent a memo to the state coordinators, national board members, and committee chairs detailing how each issue area might be used to support the fight for the ERA. Specifically, the Education Committee was instructed to concentrate on mobilizing students for the ERA by putting up tables on college campuses with ERA informational postcards. The Lesbian Rights Committee was asked to mobilize the gay community for the ERA. The Marriage and Divorce Committee was asked to plan a rally with the theme "give mom equality for Mother's Day" and to produce a fact sheet that would provide information about how the ERA would affect marriage and divorce laws. The group charged with developing a program for early childhood development created the ERA slogan "When women suffer inequality—children suffer." The Media Committee was tasked with "us[ing] personal contacts with friendly cartoonists and columnists to get publicity for ERA." The

Minority Women Committee was asked to distribute a pamphlet titled *Minority Women and ERA* and to mobilize their relatives and neighbors for the ERA in a door-to-door campaign. The Religion Committee was to "develop information on status of women in churches," despite the fact that their role in churches would not be affected by the ERA (National Organization for Women Records 1978b). Nevertheless, in 1978, fully half of the Religion Committee budget went to the ERA campaign (National Organization for Women Records 1978a).

Though money was scarce for all NOW's committees except those devoted to the ERA and abortion rights, the situation was far worse for some. In a memo to the Social Equality Committee of the national board, Mary Ellen Verheyden-Hilliard, the Education Task Force chair, wrote passionately about the importance of educational reform as a way to fix fundamental issues for both sexes across the life-span, before noting that her task force had "no budget at all during 1976–77." She noted that for the fiscal year 1975–76, she had paid all expenses herself, including "telephoning, travel (both local and to regional and national con[f]erences), paper, [and] duplication," to contribute to the broader organization. But this sort of arrangement was not sustainable; volunteers could not continue to shoulder these expenses alone. She wrote, "We need (which, I realize is not the same as being able to afford) what the NAACP has—a Director of Education. . . . We need someone full time, with a budget to develop materials, keep in constant touch with task forces and to promulgate NOW's position to outsiders—who are increasingly willing to listen on the education issue" (National Organization for Women Records, n.d.-c).

By the mid-1970s, task force leaders began advocating that they should be set free to raise their own funds directly without being required to go through the board. While the board of directors had barred task forces from raising their own money and having bank accounts, in a memo to the board in 1974, the task force leaders noted that some groups were raising their own money anyway and were not being compelled in every case to turn the money over to the national treasurer (National Organization for Women Records 1974e). The issue continued to simmer until the next year, when national task force coordinators voted for financial freedom from the board, including having access to advance money rather than having to wait for the approval process, freedom to open and freely access bank accounts specifically devoted to their issue, and freedom to keep 100 percent of money raised by a task force for its own budget (National Organization for Women Records 1975e).

There is no record that the NOW board followed through with task force leaders' suggestions, and given the board's intense focus on the ERA at the time, requests to divert money to other priorities likely hit a brick wall. Relationships between the task forces and the board were also strained when task forces could raise their own money from selling products they developed, which could instigate disputes about who could rightfully claim the proceeds. This was the case with the Consciousness Raising Committee in the late 1970s. Consciousness raising had emerged from the liberation branch of the movement and had taken hold in NOW among younger grassroots members. It became an important vehicle for NOW chapters for recruiting and training new members, but NOW leaders had remained rather resistant to institutionalizing it as an official part of the national organization (see chapter 4). This is made plain in an October 1977 letter to the board of directors' Membership Committee penned by Harriet Perl (National Organization for Women Records 1977b). Perl served as secretary for the Los Angeles NOW and as an organizer for its Consciousness Raising Committee. The committee had been a success, and Perl developed and led consciousness-raising seminars throughout the country. On the basis of her expertise, she coauthored a popular handbook, *Guidelines to Feminist Consciousness Raising*. At the national conference in 1977, NOW members voted to create a permanent national committee for consciousness raising that was "funded sufficiently to carry on a national program" ("Consciousness Raising General Resolution" in National Organization for Women, n.d.-a).

Perl, appointed to lead the new committee, and her coauthor had been selling copies of the *Guidelines*. Her letter to the board details their conflict with the board of directors over whether the national committee should be funded exclusively through the profits from the *Guidelines* and whether the book's proceeds belonged to NOW. Perl wrote,

> Asking one committee to be self-supporting while the parent organization supplies another committee with a budget is unfair on the face of it; but even worse is the spinoff which seems to follow: . . . if one group can be self-supporting, all should be, with the consequences that all committees spend time doing individual fundraisers, resulting in a fragmented organization, unwholesome competition within NOW, wasted energies—and most serious of all—loss of control of its parts by the whole organization. (National Organization for Women Records 1977b)

She concluded that the Consciousness Raising Committee should be financed from the national budget exactly as all other subunits of NOW were supported, irrespective of any possible income from the *Guidelines*. The issue continued to fester until NOW bought the copyright to the *Guidelines* from Perl and her coauthor in 1982 (Love 2006, 356).

Within NOW, other members and leaders rarely knew or cared much about any particular task force's work, even though task force policy decisions were governed by both the board and the national membership. In some cases, the task forces were simply working on issues that generated little interest among rank-and-file members, an often-heartbreaking situation for the passionate coordinators. At a meeting with NOW president Karen DeCrow in 1975, national coordinator for Women in the Arts, Suzanne Benton, argued that art had revolutionary possibilities and could change the world by offering an alternative vision for social relationships. Yet her work was hampered at every turn by national NOW's neglect for her task force. She lamented that it took months to get her task force's newsletter out, and even then, it went to few people. She wanted to establish regular contact with "every museum in the country" but couldn't get the resources to do so (National Organization for Women Records 1975e). More than anything, she wanted more autonomy to act on her task force's behalf and to control its finances. Under these circumstances, it's clear how the appeal of breaking away could sometimes trump the rewards of staying inside a powerful organization.

Leaving NOW

Prioritization of some issues over others is a necessary evil for bureaucratic organizations and NOW is no exception. For many NOW task forces and committees, which labored in isolation on the periphery, it created a fork in the road. Several membership clusters in this part of the organization decided their efforts were better directed outside of NOW in new, independent organizations.

Older Women's Task Force

Tish Sommers, who joined NOW in 1971, motivated by the plight of older women in a youth-obsessed culture, advocated for and was asked to chair a task force for these issues at the national level of NOW. But Sommers was frequently frustrated by her inability to get what she needed from the board of directors, despite her status as a board member and her role as task force coordinator. Passionate about creating a Women's Action Training Center that would train older women for employment opportunities and in how to become politically involved and effective, Sommers approached NOW for sponsorship of the center. Because it was concentrated on service provision, the center didn't easily fit into NOW's established pathways for activism, and NOW leaders proved ambivalent about moving forward with the center as a priority. Although the board of directors approved her request by a slim majority, Sommers could see the trouble she courted in trying to wring financial support in the future from an organization spread across so many issues. She declined the approval and set up a local and independent center in Oakland in 1973, free from NOW's oversight (Huckle 1991).

Sommers agreed to stay on as head of the task force on older women for national NOW, using it as a basis for advocating on a larger scale for older women's concerns. The task force connected her to thousands of women across the country, reaching out to tell their stories of how widowhood and divorce had left them struggling to support themselves. This outpouring confirmed Sommers's belief that older women could be mobilized into a political force if they were given the space and attention to unite them and train them for that work. That was never going to happen in NOW alone, given the meager resources NOW could offer the task force. So Sommers used the task force as a platform to connect to new audiences, even as she directed most of her activism toward developing new organizations outside of NOW. This work primarily took the form of the Displaced Homemakers Network and the Alliance for Displaced Homemakers (ADH), which she founded with Laurie Shields. The new groups focused on lobbying for state and federal funding for training centers for older women and on mobilizing older women for the feminist movement.

While she saw the work as complementary, Sommers's dual role as coordinator of the ADH and coordinator for the NOW task force eventually began to cause trouble with other NOW leaders. Members of the national board believed NOW was not getting enough credit for "raising consciousness on displaced-homemakers' issues" (Huckle 1991, 198). In 1977, to reconcile the competing groups, NOW re-formed her task force into the Older Women's Rights Committee, and Sommers stepped back from her role in the ADH. But, as with the other task forces, the bureaucratic reshuffling did little to amend the broader structural inequality that irritated Sommers about NOW. She struggled to get information and resources from the board, and she clashed with President Eleanor Smeal over NOW's position on age-specific language of displaced homemakers' legislation. Smeal did not want to exclude younger women, while Sommers

argued that it was the intersection of age and displacement that created the burden. As a part of NOW, Sommers was bound to the NOW
position—one she could not tolerate. Chafing at the structure that tied
her to positions with which she did not agree, she chose to leave NOW
completely. In 1978, with her activist partner Shields, Sommers began
again to plan for a new, independent organization, the Older Women's
League, which formally launched in 1980 (Huckle 1991).

Minority Women's Task Force

Similar dynamics plagued NOW's various iterations of the committee
devoted to racial equality for women of color. Although NOW has long
had a reputation for neglecting women of color, race had been a part of
NOW's core platform since the early 1970s. At the national conference in
1971, the membership voted to create a national task force on minority
women, with a particular purpose of "making coalitions with organizations of minority women to support them on common issues" (National
Organization for Women, n.d.-a). In 1973, NOW members held the first
"Black Caucus" at the national conference, and the general membership
passed a resolution to recognize that the future of the organization was
inextricably tied to the well-being of women of color. The resolution declared that NOW would eliminate the structures, policies, and practices
within NOW that inhibited the participation of minority women. As a
part of this commitment, NOW declared its intention to adopt a slid-
ing scale of dues and conference fees for economically disadvantaged
women, hold meetings in places accessible to communities of color, make
child care available at meetings, and include issues of race and racism in
consciousness-raising programs.

Despite these resolutions, the Minority Women's Committee appar-
ently languished, making little headway in achieving its goals. In 1973,
in a letter to board members, chapter presidents, and the other task force
coordinators, the Minority Women's Committee insistently declared that
the committee was "alive and functioning!!!" (Loretta J. Ross Papers 1973).
Three Californian members were taking over the job of coordinating the
task force—Patsy Fulcher, Aileen Hernandez, and Eleanor Spikes. All
three were African American, and they noted that they were looking for
help to reach out to other racial groups as well. Their letter announced
their plans to develop materials to communicate "the cultural differences" that might increase NOW's understanding of the concerns faced
by minority women.

But during the frenzied ERA campaign, the Minority Women's Committee continued to rank as a low priority. Despite its goals, and the proposals to bring more women of color into leadership, by 1977, NOW had no women of color on its national board. In 1979, NOW created a "minority outreach program" that was designed, in the words of Hernandez, to "indoctrinate minority women in why they should support the Equal Rights Amendment" rather than working for women of color directly or recruiting them to leadership positions in NOW (Loretta J. Ross Papers 1979). By 1980, Hernandez, who had long urged NOW and its board to pay greater attention to the needs and issues important to women of color, seemed to give up on NOW completely, calling for black women to boycott NOW (Loretta J. Ross Papers 1980).

Yet, long before this critical break with NOW, the three coordinators of the Minority Women's Task Force—Hernandez, Spikes, and Fulcher—had been channeling their energies into a new separate organization. In 1973, with a group of other Bay Area activists, they formed Black Women Organized for Action (BWOA), a local organization that would focus more narrowly on black women in the Bay Area, assisting them with "employment, day care, and tax preparation, and provided counseling for family violence" (LeBlanc-Ernest 2013, 98). The choice to form a new organization was driven by their realization that "black women needed an organization that combined both [feminism and black liberation] and modified them to address issues of specific concern to African American women." In other words, the founders realized that a general women's organization could never provide the targeted message and help that a local, specialist organization could. Similarly, in her work on black women's organizing, Kimberly Springer notes that Hernandez, Spikes, and Fulcher continued to work in NOW simultaneously to founding BWOA, as they "wanted explicitly to define and work on Black women's concerns, as well as to encourage Black women's leadership" throughout the feminist movement (Springer 2001, 62).

Within NOW, the consequences of its bureaucratic structure continued to be felt on the Minority Women's Committee into the 1980s. Tasked with the job to recruit women of color into NOW, Loretta Ross noted to other NOW leaders that the problem was not actually in finding women to join NOW; it was giving them something to stay for. The "revolving door" for women of color, according to Ross, happened largely because women of color were unrepresented among NOW's leaders, then based in Pittsburgh, who unofficially ran NOW. Ross (2004) explained:

They had relationships with each other, history and relationships that meant that a lot of times, the decision-making was taking place over the bridge of these relationships. It had nothing to do with what took place in the office, or what it had to do with what took place in the office. . . . Let's say we're having a staff meeting to decide on a particular course of action. Well, certain women in that meeting have already talked about this the night before over dinner, just in their normal course of being together. So, they come to the meeting kind of like as a united front, so what really looks like debate or discussion is really a smaller group of people imposing their agenda on the rest of us. And so, learning how to mark the marked and the unmarked power at NOW, and if a woman of color who doesn't have those histories, don't have those relationships, comes in, she feels like she's being victimized by forces that she can't explain.

Invoking Freeman's (1975) "Tyranny of Structurelessness," Ross pointed to the complicated ways NOW's leadership structure at the national level was both formal and informal, leaving many women, including those responsible for the actions and programs for women of color, on the periphery of the national organization's core.

In 1982, the issue reemerged after members engaged in an intense fight at the national convention to pass another resolution promoting "minority interests" in the organization. While the resolution ultimately passed, at least some members of color "felt [they] had to fight too hard to get the resolution passed and that NOW [was] growing reluctant to press for minority rights" at a time when the organization was focused on other battles. The problem of dropping in position on NOW's priority list spurred discussion among black women at the conference of "forming their own African American feminist group" (Cummings 1982). There is no evidence that this group split, but it remains obvious that women of color continued to be frustrated by their peripheral position in the organization and pondered whether it might be better to go their own way.

Splitting the Legal Committee

The challenges of priority setting naturally led to disagreements about how to prioritize financial resources among the task forces, including thorny questions about task forces raising money independently from NOW and their autonomy in spending decisions. Task forces were restricted from raising their own money and didn't have access to independent bank accounts that they could access without first going through the board. In 1973, the budget for each task force was only $100 for administrative costs. The task force status report in July of that year makes it plain that this was simply not enough to effectively run their programs. Some task force leaders were routinely "forced to draw from their own funds or simply forgo providing assistance to chapters" when they had run out of money (National Organization for Women Records 1973).

This problem was acute for all task forces, even among those that were prioritized by the board of directors. The organizational structure isolated most of the task forces from the board, at least to some degree. Combined with the constant financial stress, this isolation resulted in membership splits on even the most critical task forces. For example, in 1968, the Legal Committee was swamped with NOW's highest-profile work—representing women in several prominent discrimination lawsuits against major corporations. The cases required a considerable financial commitment from the NOW board, and NOW founders had planned to quickly split off a separate legal defense fund that would operate independently and be able to accept tax-exempt donations to support its work (see chapter 6). By 1968, the independent legal fund had still not been incorporated, and the Legal Committee began to break under the strain of overwork and lack of money. Marguerite Rawalt, a retired lawyer serving as the head of the Legal Committee, was responsible for signing all court briefs filed on behalf of NOW. Because she was retired, her career was not at risk by publicly acknowledging her activist role in NOW. While other members of the committee did a great deal of the work, they were still employed by government agencies and could not be publicly associated with NOW. The Legal Committee worked on the cases at a frantic pace, and Rawalt was often required to sign documents without time to read them or make changes (Banaszak 2010; Eastwood 1992).

Tensions over the pace and volume of work were made worse by the lack of money. The committee desperately needed to hire additional administrative help. In the years before the legal fund was formed, the minutes from NOW's board of directors meetings are replete with desperate pleas from the Legal Committee for greater financial support from NOW leaders (National Organization for Women Records 1967a). Faith Seidenberg, vice president of legal affairs, declared:

> If we are to continue our legal work, however, we are going to need money. I realize that everything we do in NOW is important . . . [but] we cannot continue to take cases in the name of NOW unless we have, at the very least, case expenses. (National Organization for Women Records 1970)

Given the desperate state of affairs, everyone agreed that a separate 501(c)(3) legal defense organization to handle the cases was necessary. But leaders struggled to get it off the ground, and turf wars erupted between the board of directors and the Legal Committee over how independent the new organization should actually be, or if, as the proposed bylaws stated, the membership organization's Legal Committee would "be in direct control of any litigation endorsed by the fund" (cited in Banaszak 2010, 103). Members of the Legal Committee also fought with each other and with the board over who would be on the new board of directors and who would stay in NOW. At a 1968 NOW meeting in which the board of directors was asked to vote who would become staff in the new organization, the Legal Committee disintegrated.

Marguerite Rawalt resigned, leaving no attorney in NOW who could attach her name to the cases NOW was backing. With the Legal Committee in chaos and uncertain how to move forward, May Eastwood and Caruthers Berger, another committee member, ventured outside of NOW. They committed their personal money to continue the discrimination cases and sought the help of famed suffragette Alice Paul. Paul agreed to help pay the costs to continue the cases to ensure that they would not be dropped, writing her check in Berger's name rather than NOW's. The logistical problem of what to do with the check gave the two lawyers the impetus to split away from NOW completely and take the discrimination cases with them. They created a bank account for the new organization, eventually settling on the name Human Rights for Women, and began the process of securing tax exemption for their new legal organization (Eastwood 1992).

At its heart, the split on the Legal Committee was driven by organizational problems in the bureaucratic structure—little autonomy, few resources, and too many projects. The passionate members of the Legal Committee could not let the women they represented pay the price for these problems. In leaving, they found greater freedom to raise money and to concentrate on the particular kinds of activism for which they were both passionate and skilled.

Passion Projects and External Pressures

Languishing in NOW's periphery created one incentive to break away. There were other reasons to leave as well. Although NOW was a household name, and indisputably a dominant force in the feminist movement,

NOW's reputation could also be an albatross for task forces and committees in trying to collaborate with outside actors.

An important part of task force work was building coalitions with other groups, outside of NOW, who were working on similar issues. Arriving in collaborations as representatives of NOW, a behemoth in the feminist movement, made some relationships difficult or impossible. Sometimes task force members sought ways to disguise their actual membership and found it easier to accomplish their work without NOW's name behind them.

Task Force on Religion

In the mid-1960s, young theologian Elizabeth Farians was growing increasingly unsettled by the discrimination she faced from men in the Catholic community. She had always been smart and a devoted Catholic. After teaching for a few years, Farians decided to make a deeper commitment to the Church and to its mission for social justice by pursuing a doctorate in theology. But the discrimination she faced in trying to participate in Catholic academic societies convinced her that the Catholic Church and other patriarchal religions should be reformed to recognize women's contributions. In 1966, Farians read about NOW's founding in the press and reached out to Friedan, who recruited her to NOW by offering her control of a newly created task force on women in religion. Farians quickly agreed.

But life inside of NOW came at a cost. Representing a feminist organization made it easy for religious authorities to ignore Farians's task force. Catholic bishops would only consent to meet with Catholic groups, fundamentally ruling out any formal conversation with NOW's ecumenical task force on religion. Even to get a meeting with Church authorities, Farians had to create something new, outside of NOW. She reached out to six other Catholic women's groups, including the Deaconess Movement, the women's rights committee of the National Association of Laymen, St. Joan's International Alliance, the National Coalition of American Nuns, and Women Theologians United, inviting them to join a new group. She then created a Catholic Caucus within NOW's task force, adding it to the list of Catholic women's organizations that would come together under a new name. They called their new group Joint Committee of Organizations Concerned with the Status of Women in the Church (JCO) (Elizabeth Farians Papers 1972).

Branching outside of NOW filled a critical need for the Catholic women who couldn't meet their goals from inside of NOW. When asked how other NOW leaders felt about the task force extending into a new organization, Farians (telephone interview with the author, June 25, 2009) laughed, "Oh, I don't think they cared what we did one way or another. . . . [NOW's] main interest was employment and whatever the other major women's problems were at the time." Because religion was not a main focus in NOW, Farians's task force was neglected, but it was also free to do whatever it wanted, including dropping NOW's name when it proved inconvenient.

Building a new, external organization also created additional coalition opportunities for the task force that would have been impossible from within NOW. Many of the organizations that partnered with the Catholic Caucus were filled with women who would have never joined or partnered with NOW proper. NOW's stand in favor of abortion rights was an affront to conservative women in general and created trouble in recruiting devout Catholic women who might otherwise be sympathetic to a feminist worldview.

More generally, many of the other Catholic groups were uncomfortable with NOW's confrontational nature; they preferred a softer pressure that was a better fit for the particulars of the Catholic faith. Some of them simply wanted a greater role for the laity of the church. Others were subtly pushing for women's ordination. St. Joan's International Alliance's position, for example, was "whenever the church is willing to consider the ordination of women, we will be waiting and ready and willing to serve" (Farians, interview). In forming the Joint Committee, Farians recruited other women to lead the group from anti-abortion Catholic groups. Their leadership communicated to the external world, and more importantly to the Catholic Church, that while the Catholic Caucus from NOW was a member, the committee itself was distinct from NOW's more radical politics. In 1970, with a group of exclusively Catholic members, they were finally able to secure a meeting with American bishops to press their demands.

In 1972, Farians was fired from her job as a theology professor at Loyola University because of her criticism of the church. In dire financial straits, she stepped back from the feminist movement to concentrate on supporting herself. With her went much of the fire for Catholic activism in NOW, and many of the Catholic caucus members left the organization shortly after. Three local New York NOW members, Joan Harriman, Patricia Fogarty McQuillan, and Meta Mulcahey, wanted to continue the tradition of Catholic feminist activism, while not hiding their support for reproductive rights. They decided to form a new group, Catholics for a Free Choice, eventually renamed Catholics for Choice (CFC). Many women who had been in NOW joined the new organization, and many stayed active in both organizations. They saw the need for both kinds of feminist work, recognizing that CFC could do things NOW simply could not. According to Mary Jean Collins, who served as both NOW's task force coordinator and on the board of directors for CFC, McQuillan knew that "the issue would never become the highest priority within a generalist organization, and she felt it needed to be given direct attention. . . . NOW would never understand the Catholic Church the way she did and understand how the fights had to be undertaken. . . . That wasn't going to happen from NOW" (Collins, interview). With the founding of CFC, NOW was only too happy to have an independent ally of feminist Catholics in the broader feminist movement. The work could be done and the resources raised by the new group, and the feminist movement could be expanded to new domains.

NOW's task force for women in politics experienced similar circumstances before a core group of its members broke away. In the early 1970s, NOW leaders and members were divided on how invested NOW should be in mainstream politics. Several founders and influential leaders, including presidents Betty Friedan and Karen DeCrow, were passionate about getting women involved in institutional politics at all levels—local, state, and federal. They pressed for the creation of a task force that would focus on preparing women to run for office and on lobbying politicians to support women's issues.

Even with NOW's heavy hitters involved in the task force, they faced strong resistance to their agenda. Most NOW members knew little and cared little about politics (National Organization for Women Records 1975e). They wanted NOW to stay an outside agitator, putting pressure on politicians and elites through their activism in the streets. Friedan countered that institutional politics was centrally important for gaining women's equality; it could not just be forfeited by women's organizations. In any case, NOW's tax-exempt status prevented the membership organization from endorsing candidates, and members and leaders continued to resist the idea of starting a separate political action committee (but see chapter 6). These barriers in NOW crippled the task force, and its leaders recognized that their energies would be better spent on a new organization completely independent from NOW (Collins 2009).

Tired of trying to get NOW to support the task force's political agenda, in 1971, Friedan and several other national leaders began partnering with people outside of NOW, including Bella Abzug and Gloria Steinem, to begin the National Women's Political Caucus (NWPC) (DeCrow 1981; Farians 1997; Tully 1992). Unlike NOW, the NWPC was narrowly devoted to getting women nominated within the two major political parties and was organized to be broadly inclusive of both liberal and conservative women. In this way, like CFC, the NWPC's founding offered a fresh perspective in the movement and attracted women who would not have joined NOW (M. Fox, telephone interview with the author, June 1, 2009).

Conclusion

Many new organizations started as part of NOW, and their exit from it represented not a failure but a healthy expansion of feminist ideas and identities. In 1991, in her oral history of NOW, Gene Boyer noted that the feminist movement needed diversity and that dividing into new organizations, from her view, was a good thing for everyone involved:

> The proliferation of organizations that has occurred around issues of the women's movement proves each group, each constituency, does need that thinking-[through] with like-minded people of similar backgrounds and experiences in order to articulate their particular issues. . . . Each one of these caucuses, whether they be ethnic caucuses, like Asian-American women, African-American women, native American women, or vocational caucuses like women in arts, women in sports, women in academia, women in business, they each have their own program to develop, their own set of feminist principles and rights to articulate; and then they also have a stake in the larger context, such as the Equal Rights Amendment.

Boyer, like many NOW leaders over the past decades, understood and prioritized feminist gains beyond the walls of her own organization. The movement needed separate spaces, where those activists passionate about particular issues could focus exclusively on achieving a narrow set of goals. This was inherently positive, and schism, in that sense, was an important part of how the feminist movement developed. Everything did not need to happen under one organizational roof. Yet, even if schisms provide benefits to broader movements, they are often still painful for the members involved.

As with local chapters, the majority of NOW's task forces and committees were operating at the periphery of NOW's structure. This gave them immense freedom to engage in the kinds of projects and identity construction they wanted. A core part of the task forces' and committees' mission was to engage with the outside world on behalf of NOW in ways that made the world better for women. Acting as the face of NOW when interacting with foundations, churches, universities, politicians, museums—the list goes on and on—task force members carried the benefits of that affiliation. But they also sometimes paid a price. NOW may have been in the more mainstream wing of the feminist movement, but for many of these external actors, NOW was as radical as any other feminist group. Sometimes being in NOW created trouble because it gave task force members too high a profile, raising hackles before they could accomplish anything. Under these conditions, task forces were forced to reconsider the value of being a peripheral player in an organization that cost them so much in their external relationships. Wasn't it possible that they could accomplish more if they were freed from NOW's reputation and could pursue resources and partnerships on their own terms? For at least some, the answer to this question was yes—breaking away was clearly the right choice.

Though NOW's task force structure spawned many new organizations in the 1970s and 1980s, the pace of splits seems to have slowed in the 1990s and 2000s. It is difficult to know for sure, as not every new group advertises its roots in a previous one. Because of this, it is impossible to definitively say how many groups formed this way in the past or how many might still be using this path to build new organizations. But there is good reason to believe that this pattern of breaking away has become less common over time.

First, while NOW continues to be a generalist organization, it has explicitly narrowed its national public agenda to a handful of issues. Its more specific focus does not preclude actions or positions being taken on a wider range of topics, but it also likely lowers the expectations of committee members that those more specific topics should receive equal energy and money and thus likely reduces the pressure to break away when they do not get a spotlight.

Second, the broader political and cultural environment grew more conservative in the 1980s and 1990s—a change that was undeniably a problem for feminist organizing. In this context, it is also likely that even those members who wished they were getting more resources in their current organization would have been less optimistic about their chances of making it on their own, particularly with a very narrowly focused specialist organization. Thus, in the past few decades, the pressures that pushed some task force members to break away have now reversed, creating greater incentives for factions to stay inside their large and stable general-ist organization or simply to leave the movement altogether.

The process of splitting through task forces does not fit our typical narrative about how schisms happen. In NOW, there were sometimes hard feelings between those who left and those who stayed, and some of these feelings have softened over time as activists look back with more clarity and perspective about events leading up to the splits. But it is also clear that the underlying causes of the splits were not deep ideological or tactical divides, or personality conflicts, between leaders. Instead, they were often more mundane conflicts emerging from routine organizational struggles. Most often the fights were about the lack of organizational time, energy, and money to do everything well. Even as it created conflicts among members, NOW's bureaucratic structure also allowed it to grow into the largest feminist organization in the United States and sustain its operations even during hostile political and cultural environments. Its generalist approach allowed it to maintain itself over time as issues came in and out of fashion. And, most importantly, rather than dampening in-novation and creativity, its structure gave its members room to take on new issues, to experiment, and to innovate new strategies.

This freedom also created the conditions for passionate members, de-voted to a single issue, to find each other, create unique collective identi-ties, and, ultimately, to branch out on their own. In this way, organiza-tional splitting through task forces represents a form of schism, in that it would not have happened without internal discord and dissatisfaction within the organization. But it also represents a positive new chapter for both NOW and the new groups that form from NOW's task forces. I re-turn to the challenges and benefits of these relationships in the conclusion.

In the next chapter, I examine the ways NOW has consciously reached beyond its boundaries, extending its bureaucracy to a broader system of organizational spin-offs. Whereas these splits were driven by pragmatic concerns about fund-raising and regulations, I investigate how the splits led to conflict and factionalism after the separation.

CHAPTER SIX

Splitting Satellites

Nonprofit Status and Schism in Social Movements

In 1970, after years of infighting and financial distress on its Legal Committee, NOW created the NOW Legal Defense and Education Fund (LDEF; later renamed Legal Momentum), an organization that would be able to accept tax-exempt donations from donors and foundations. By 1977, NOW had further divided its functions to include a national political action committee (PAC) and a system of state-level PACs for lower-level feminist candidates. In 1986, NOW formed the NOW Foundation, with the mission to raise money for NOW's feminist educational campaigns. Each of these new divisions is a legally distinct organization, with its own governing system, goals, and, most importantly, state-sanctioned ways of independently raising money. Even NOW's state-level chapters have created separate foundations to support their local work. By creating satellite organizations, NOW transformed from a single-membership organization into an organizational system, with the membership group operating as its controlling center and each new satellite group fulfilling a specific, peripheral function. NOW's not alone in dividing this way; Sierra Club, for example, has created a notably elaborate system, including a membership organization, an educational foundation, a student coalition, a PAC, and a publishing arm.

These examples of bureaucratic division are a part of a broader trend in the advocacy sector. Since the 1970s and 1980s, the United States has seen a boom in both membership groups and "memberless" organizations. In contrast to membership associations, which mobilize individual members into activist and civic organizations, memberless organizations are "public law groups, think tanks, foundations, and political action committees" (Skocpol 2004). A large literature has developed in the effort to understand the causes and consequences of these different kinds of organizations, with particular concern that memberless groups are replacing membership groups. Despite this fear, Walker, McCarthy, and Baumgartner (2011) found that these organizational forms develop together—rather than competing, they represent distinct organizational repertoires that serve complementary functions in a social movement (see also Akchurin and Lee 2013; McCarthy and Walker 2004). These organizational types do not just develop de novo; they often emerge as the satellite organizations of membership groups.

In NOW, the decision to create these new organizations did not come from thorny ideological or personality disputes; instead, it seems NOW leaders unanimously agreed that the organization needed to develop a peripheral set of separate organizations that would operate semi-independently. In fact, they merely saw it as one further elaboration of the existing bureaucracy—a slight differentiation of roles that would allow everyone to more easily do the jobs they were already doing. However, this view of the organizational shift did not work out seamlessly. In fact, it produced surprising factionalism and carried consequences no one anticipated at the outset.

Across the political spectrum, many formalized social movement groups are, legally speaking, actually systems of independent organizations, sharing a name and a general mission, while carrying out distinct functions, with a distinct message, for distinct audiences. At the same time, satellite groups are crafted to work closely, even indistinguishably, from a parent organization. They are often referred to as the "legal arm," or sister organizations to the better-known membership organization. But these labels imply a mutual, equal relationship that does not quite fit their arrangement. I prefer the term *satellite group* because it better captures the structural inequality built into the relationship. As we will see, satellite groups are peripheralized in ways that can provoke factionalism and produce deeper organizational splits than leaders originally intended.

This pattern of organizational splitting fits neatly with the bureaucratic capacity to divide functions into core and peripheral clusters. As discussed briefly in chapter 2, movement organizations create new satellites to comply with external authorities and state policies. Creating a new group can also help craft a slightly differentiated organizational identity that is better suited to attract support from elites and foundations. All movement groups interact with these environmental forces to some degree, and splitting into legally separate entities is a common response to these routine pressures (Reid 2006). Because bureaucratic movement organizations are often large with diverse memberships, they must find ways to manage many simultaneous and conflicting demands for particular goals, ideologies, and tactics. This problem is compounded by their constant need to raise money for new projects and routine maintenance. Dues are an important source of support that keep members invested in the organization, but outside donations can offer greater flexibility in renewing programs, building reserves, and moving in new directions. Nonprofit tax policy makes meeting these needs difficult—members often want to engage in explicitly political activism, but donors often prefer tax-exempt organizations, which have tight restrictions on the kinds of political work in which they can engage. By splitting, the core membership organization can maintain a relatively more aggressive agenda, while the peripheral satellite group can cultivate a more reserved reputation in compliance with external rules and donor preferences.

The decision to split off some functions into peripheral organizations is straightforward. However, the consequences of the splitting are not always clear at the outset. Leaders in the parent and the satellite group plan on a close working relationship, collaborating much as they had before. But the structure of their relationships has changed, introducing new sources of tension, and even factionalism, between the closely allied groups. Leaders in both groups are forced to repeatedly negotiate which group represents the organizational brand, which should get credit for successful campaigns, and which should get blamed for bad press. These problems are compounded as the organizations drift further from each other, driven by their different needs, different audiences, and distinct visions.

Satellite organizations are not typically categorized as organizational splitting because they are intentionally and pragmatically created. But when we think of them as simple spin-offs, or different versions of the same organization, we are not able to see how the unequal structure of their relationship seeds conflict and factionalism or how those conflicts are shaped by the broader social movement field. Their distinct collective identities, cultures, and audiences reinforce their diverging trajectories, pushing them further apart from each other. In this space, friction grows between the parent and the satellite over whether and how to maintain a coherent shared agenda.

Division of Labor and Nonprofit Status in Social Movements

Nonprofit organizations are "self-governing organizations that do not distribute profits to those who control them and are exempt from federal income taxes by virtue of being organized for public purposes" (Boris 2006, 3). Nonprofits over a certain size are required to register with the state, and advocacy organizations that wish to claim a nonprofit status must abide by the rules established by the IRS, the Federal Election Commission, and state governments. Large social movement groups are generally incorporated with the IRS as 501(c)(4) nonprofit groups, allowing them to engage in some political advocacy on behalf of their members, including minimal electioneering, political lobbying, and partisan communication with members, without paying taxes on their income. However, a 501(c)(4) designation prevents donors to these groups from deducting their gifts from their own taxes, making them less attractive to large donors and foundations. Even with this trade-off, the amount of political activity they are allowed to conduct is limited and cannot be the primary purpose of the organization.[1] Other groups incorporate with the IRS under the 501(c)(3) guidelines, forgoing political advocacy altogether and allowing donors to deduct their gifts. Tax-exempt organizations, particularly those with the designation 501(c)(3), are considered "charitable" organizations and, as such, are not allowed to engage in most kinds of advocacy. To engage in extensive and explicit political activity, organizations must register as PACs, known as 527 groups.

McCarthy, Britt, and Wolfson (1991) argue that tax regulations work to channel organizations into less threatening and contentious activities due to the pressure to retain the tax-exempt benefits. However appealing tax-exempt status is, it places considerable limits on a group's choice in tactics, stripping them of some of their most powerful tools for social change by limiting their political influence. But social movement groups are inherently political—their aim, after all, is not just to raise money but to effect real change in the political world.

In response to the dilemma of how to register with the state, many large membership groups have expanded their bureaucratic structures by

---

1 From NOW Legal Defense and Education Fund Records (n.d.-a, 2): "What activities are not eligible for Fund Support? The Fund cannot adopt projects which engage in efforts to change laws, or publish materials which might be interpreted as encouraging or exhorting people to exert pressure to influence the outcome of legislations. It must be impartial and objective in that it cannot advocate a position or take action on a clearly controversial issue or in a partisan manner. The Fund can seek to discover, explain and disseminate facts, and provide educational background on issues and legal rights, but it cannot tell people what to do about their conclusions, how to act upon their opinions, or prod them to campaign for an objective which can be obtained only by legislation."

deploying some of their professional leaders to run satellite organizations. In splitting into multiple, closely networked organizations, movement groups incorporate the benefits of multiple organizational repertoires under a single identity umbrella (Clemens 1993; Walker and McCarthy 2010). The only way to engage in a broad range of political, educational, and charitable activities without risking the benefits of tax exemption is to slice these functions off, creating peripheral satellites with specialized functions and tactics (Boris 2006; Reid 2006).

NOW leaders plainly stated this position in the early 1970s, when explaining to members why they had to form a new, distinct organization. Their explanation to members laid out the benefits of a 501(c)(3) designation:

> Foundations, Government Agencies, Corporations and most Individuals do not give grants or sizeable charitable gifts to individuals; they give to organized groups. And in most cases they will not give to just any group. They give to groups organized for educational, scientific or charitable purposes and groups which are both tax exempt and can receive tax-deductible contributions. (NOW Legal Defense and Education Fund Records, n.d.-a, 1)

Later, when NOW divided again to include a 527 PAC, leaders similarly explained their choice in the introduction to the first NOW/PAC manual, writing, "In order to avoid having to divert NOW energy to interpreting [tax-exemption] law, having to defend our actions, or having to open our books for IRS inspection, it is easier to avoid the problem by simply creating a Political Action Committee (PAC)" (National Organization for Women Records 1979b).

The relationships between the organizations are also subject to other restrictions. Theoretically, each organization is legally separate and cannot share day-to-day operations with any of the other groups in the system. In practice, however, they are often enmeshed to the point of being indistinguishable. The groups can have overlapping boards of directors as well as collaborate on goals and strategies. To some extent, they can also share financial resources. For example, a charitable 501(c)(3) organization can give money to an advocacy 501(c)(4) organization as long as the money does not go to support the activities in which the 501(c)(3) cannot itself engage, like partisan advocacy. But of course, any money from the 501(c)(3) frees up other resources in the 501(c)(4) to devote to political endeavors.

These sorts of organizational arrangements have been criticized for their lack of transparency and the difficulty outsiders have in untangling the relationships between the groups (Reid 2006). But there has been little effort to investigate how the structure of their relationship shapes the groups themselves—or the conflicts between them. In NOW, satellite groups were created to be virtually indistinguishable from the core membership organization. Yet, over time, its LDEF has drifted further from NOW's core, introducing room for significant conflict and factionalism. NOW is not alone in experiencing this drift; both Sierra Club and the NAACP have experienced similar rifts with their own satellite groups. Importantly, these groups' histories also provide strategies for how these factionalizing pressures can be minimized.

NOW Legal Defense and Education Fund, Foundation, and Political Action Committees

The precursor to NOW's first 501(c)(3) division was its internal Legal Committee, created by the founding board of directors. Despite its national prominence, NOW was chronically short on financial resources, and despite its central position among NOW's priorities, the Legal Committee was forced to compete with other task forces and committees for funding (see chapter 5). To secure a more stable base of funding, the NOW board of directors agreed to establish a 501(c)(3) organization that could raise tax-exempt money to support its legal work. Accordingly, the LDEF's stated purposes were to provide legal services for women, conduct research and publish reports on discrimination, and supply legal counsel to discrimination victims. To launch the organization, several key leaders from NOW's Legal Committee transitioned from NOW to steer the new organization. Abiding by the regulations for their tax-exempt status, the LDEF's bylaws included a provision that at least some of the LDEF's leaders should not come from NOW (NOW Legal Defense and Education Fund Records 1970, 2).

While state regulations required distance between the two organizations, leaders in both groups wanted the LDEF to closely align with NOW and to raise money that could help both organizations. The new organization was constructed to fit closely with NOW's core membership organization, including an interlocking board of directors. The LDEF's bylaws were written so that NOW retained a high degree of power in their relationship—originally, the board of directors for the LDEF included the NOW president, chair of the national board, and the legal vice president (NOW Legal Defense and Education Fund Records 1970, 2).[2] Furthermore, the NOW board of directors and the NOW action vice president has significant veto power over which projects the LDEF could fund (NOW Legal Defense and Education Fund Records, n.d.-a, 3). Yet leaders struggled from the beginning to find the balance between maintaining a single NOW brand identity and representing their increasingly distinct and diverging interests.

While everyone on NOW's board of directors agreed that creating a separate legal organization was the right decision, they were also less than interested in the work that this new organization would do. "The LDEF was a sideshow, naturally," according to Mary Jean Tully (1992, 112). "[It's] not the activist arm, and [NOW] was an activist organization." Its development received little attention from NOW leadership, and in its original formation, the organization "existed primarily on paper."

The LDEF board met only during the breaks of NOW board meetings, when the NOW board members who were on the LDEF board were available.[3] This sometimes meant that LDEF meetings were convened in the very early morning hours, and that NOW leaders who held joint positions in both organizations failed to show up. Before it had secured its own funding, NOW gave the LDEF little financial assistance for infrastructure or day-to-day operations. Remembering the early days of the LDEF, Mary Jean Tully (1992, 58–59) recounts,

> It wasn't very important to anybody else. Nobody had ever done anything with the organization. . . . There was no staff. There was no office. There was no plan for [fund-]raising; there was no plan for spending money; the organization was in sort of limbo.

Tully served as the LDEF president from 1971 to 1977 and, along with Marilyn Hall Patel, the NOW legal vice president, made it her mission to reform it into a stronger and more independent organization. Through her prodding, NOW leaders finally gave her the resources to create a staff and begin earnestly soliciting donors for the LDEF. By the end of Tully's tenure as president, the organization had an operating budget of

2 "The members of the Fund shall consist of all current Officers and Members of the National Board of Directors of the National Organization for Women and the current Members of the Board of Directors of the Fund" (NOW Legal Defense and Education Fund Records 1970, 2).

3 The bylaws required that fund meetings occur at the NOW national conferences, although the directors and the members could call for additional meetings (NOW Legal Defense and Education Fund Records 1970).

$650,000 a year, two offices in New York City and Washington, D.C., and roughly a dozen staff (Tully 1992). To be sure, the LDEF's rising profile was a net positive for both organizations, and they worked closely toward common goals. But as the LDEF grew into a full-fledged and increasingly independent organization, new strains were introduced.

Most often, it was the structural ambiguity in the relationship between the LDEF and NOW that caused headaches to both organizations. They competed with each other in a common pool for donors who were generally interested in women's progress and equality. The overlap between the two organizations, in both name and mission, made this competition even more uncertain. Donors who had given to one of them were hesitant to give to the other, feeling like they had already given NOW money. Recognizing this problem, officers met in 1979 in an attempt to disentangle their roles. Leaders agreed that "the problems in relationship between NOW and the LDEF are competition for money . . . and the tendency of organizations to become self-serving. We must be aware of these potentialities and combat them with renewed commitment and constant awareness of our mutuality of goals." Despite the "mutuality" of their goals and the admonishment to both against tendencies to be self-serving, NOW officers also left little room for questioning what the LDEF role would be compared to its own:

> NOW [the membership organization] is the women's movement—a grassroots organization developed out of a national conception of need. . . . LDEF is a support mechanism—a grey eminence behind the scenes, helping in the need to grasp more money. LDEF can be most supportive through fundraising, organizing and leadership development . . . complementing the role of NOW. (NOW Legal Defense and Education Fund Records 1979)

Whereas NOW leaders viewed the LDEF as its "fund-raising arm," LDEF leaders insisted on an independent mission and culture. For the LDEF, this was a critical distinction, necessary to protect its tax-exempt status. In an undated letter to the NOW board of directors, Marilyn Hall Patel reminded NOW leaders that the two groups were "distinctly separate" and that the LDEF was not bound by the mandates set by NOW's members at its national conferences. LDEF leaders' primary responsibility, she insisted, was to protect the fund's "precious tax-deductible status" that helped them raise money that would be irreplaceable should the group lose its nonprofit status (NOW Legal Defense and Education Fund Records, n.d.-b, 1).

At the same time, Patel and other LDEF leaders recognized that the distinction could not so simple; there was significant overlap in the leadership between the two organizations, and those LDEF members who were also NOW officers *were* bound to NOW's conference resolutions. The interlocks between the two groups meant that LDEF leaders were often compelled to act "in a manner consistent with National Conference directives" of the membership organization when they were working with the LDEF (NOW Legal Defense and Education Fund Records, n.d.-b, 2). This balancing act was fraught, particularly in the 1970s. The NOW membership organization was being pushed in a more radical direction by its younger members, and LDEF leaders were asked both to honor those more aggressive strategies and to protect the LDEF's relationships with conservative and institutional outsiders.

The extent of this problem became clear just as the LDEF was struggling to establish itself as an important player in litigation on behalf of women's rights. To get started, they needed to compete for grants with external funding institutions. In 1975, after cultivating connections at the Ford Foundation, the LDEF was awarded $150,000 in matching grant money to help start its litigation program (Toni Carabillo and Judith Meuli Papers 1991). But to accept the money, NOW leaders had to agree to the condition that the Ford Foundation would have some level of oversight in the LDEF's operations. According to Tully (1992, 63), Ford set up oversight committees when it gave money for civil rights litigation grants to ensure that "there wouldn't be any frivolous litigation." Although this was standard operating procedure for Ford, and LDEF leaders accepted this condition without concern, "the NOW board wouldn't swallow [it]. . . . They claimed that the Ford Foundation would be deciding what we were going to be litigating, which wasn't the case." Tully pleaded with the board to reverse its decision, but it steadfastly refused to allow the LDEF to accept a grant that would mean surrendering NOW's authority over the LDEF's work. The LDEF was caught between the power-wielding membership organization and the professional demands of an external funding institution. Ultimately, its leaders were unable to persuade NOW that the conditions were worth bearing, and the LDEF declined the grant.

NOW's decision to block the grant was costly to both organizations. The LDEF had to find other ways to raise money, delaying its ability to litigate on behalf of women for years. Refusing money for the LDEF came with attendant losses to NOW because the LDEF could have funded some of NOW's nonpolitical programs. In a telling portion of her oral history, Tully argues that NOW leaders forced the LDEF to turn down the grant because NOW felt that the "LD[E]F was trying to be too separate" from NOW and that they were right about the LDEF's desire to create a distinct identity (Tully 1992, 65).

The LDEF's and NOW's different organizational cultures also meant they had conflicting strategies over how to pursue even the goals they had in common. For example, while the two organizations were equally interested in the Equal Rights Amendment (ERA) passage and frequently cooperated on projects for its passage, NOW leaders sometimes asserted control over the joint campaign in ways that were harmful to the LDEF. In one particularly important episode, the LDEF needed to send a fund-raising letter to potential supporters to raise much-needed operating money. Because Betty Friedan was a national figure and synonymous with women's struggle for equality, the LDEF's Gene Boyer asked for Friedan to sign her name to the letter. Rather than acknowledging their joint interests and complying with the request, a brash and demanding Friedan told Boyer that she would only sign the letter if the money raised would be devoted to a specific ERA campaign. After Boyer argued with her that the letter did not promise that the money would all go to the ERA and that the LDEF was desperate for operating money, Friedan exploded. At a joint fund-raiser between NOW and the LDEF, Friedan harangued Boyer in front of donors:

> Instead of giving the little "boost the fund" speech, what she did
> instead in front of this group, was take me to task about the . . . content of the letter. . . . She wanted all the money we were going to raise
> with that direct mail letter ear-marked for her ERA project. (Boyer
> 1991, 60)

In the end, the LDEF was pressured into giving part of the money raised for the LDEF to the ERA project to keep the peace with NOW and Friedan.

The LDEF's connection to NOW was costly in other ways as well, especially when the LDEF was held responsible by its sponsors for NOW's actions. For example, at a time when the LDEF was working on a wide range of gender discrimination cases, but the work was all pro bono, the young organization was in need of office space but had no budget. To acquire the needed resources, LDEF leaders courted foundations and external benefactors until the organization could begin generating fees through the court cases. In a generous act of sponsorship, in the mid-1970s, the Avon Corporation offered free New York office space to the LDEF, where they could manage their day-to-day operations. The relationship was working well, until Eleanor Smeal, president of NOW at the time, sent a fund-raising letter to members in which she criticized the Catholic Church. According to Muriel Fox, a group of "anti-feminists" threatened to organize a boycott of Avon for its support of NOW. Even though the offending actions had been taken by NOW, not the LDEF, neither the public nor the media had ever been good at distinguishing between the two. The LDEF was held jointly responsible, and Avon asked the organization to vacate its loaned offices.

The trouble between NOW and the newly formed LDEF did not end there. As the new organization developed on a different trajectory than the NOW membership organization, differences in their operating styles became a point of conflict. Mary Jean Collins, an early member of NOW's national board, remembers that NOW members were concerned about the LDEF chasing corporate money and how this impinged its ability to independently pursue women's legal and economic interests. In her interview of Tully, Mary Jean Collins noted that NOW increasingly cast the LDEF as a "sort of corporate entity" that would be remolded by the institutions they were trying to change (Tully 1992, 82).

If NOW leaders were sometimes suspicious of the LDEF, the LDEF was frequently embarrassed by what was happening in the membership organization and worried about what NOW would do to the LDEF's organizational image. When asked about the relationship between NOW and the LDEF, Tully (1992, 133) made it clear that it was sometimes a struggle to maintain their partnership:

> To be blunt about it, we wanted to distance ourselves from them, because we thought they were behaving in an often irrational way; and we were just calmer, more conservative, and more establishment than they were. We felt that they were an embarrassment, and we wanted to create a whole different image. And we did.

In contrasting the culture of the LDEF to NOW, she uses adjectives like calmer, conservative, and establishment. She also says that the NOW membership organization was sometimes an embarrassment to the leaders in the LDEF. Tully points to the heart of the organizational dilemma created when NOW spun off the 501(c)(3) organization—the two organizations were structurally linked, but they needed fundamentally different things to achieve their distinct organizational missions. As a membership organization, NOW needed to foster an activist identity, one that would mobilize members and advocate for fundamental social change. The LDEF needed to foster a quiet, professional image that would not scare away big donors and foundations in the funding environment. These relationships were critical for raising money for the operating costs that NOW could not provide, but they also created tension with NOW about what the LDEF was becoming. They were on fundamentally different trajectories, driven apart by distinct organizational needs and cultures.

At its founding, many of the more conservative and professional women in NOW had moved into the LDEF. The transfer of these kinds of activists from the member organization into the legal organization set the two organizations on different paths, making the groups less likely to find common ground in solutions. Gene Boyer started as a leader in NOW but eventually moved into leadership of the LDEF because of how different its internal culture was from NOW's. Under Tully's leadership, the LDEF cultivated a professional collective identity, putting it at odds with the leaders managing NOW, who were pressing the slogan "out of the mainstream, into the revolution." Of this fraught period, Boyer (1991, 219–20) remarked:

> [Tully] saw to it there were sociologists and psychologists and lawyers [in the LDEF]. The bylaws call for a certain number of lawyers, but these were people who had not necessarily come up through the ranks of NOW leadership. They were picked from the wider society because of their expertise, which was a very intelligent way of creating that organization. But then [the LDEF] began to have its own persona.

Boyer also highlighted the structural ambiguity for the LDEF, as it built a distinct identity: "It's not totally separate but certainly [it is] an organization with a different image, and a different mission than the membership organization. It has its own set of followers, so to speak." While they shared common goals about gender equality, their different organizational interests and experiences led to NOW being typed as confrontational and radical and the LDEF maligned as conservative and corporate.

Throughout the 1970s, as NOW was being torn apart by the rift on its board of directors (see chapter 4), the LDEF had good reason to keep NOW at arm's length. The LDEF worked to create a quiet, professional public image—a safe organization to which funders could donate large amounts of money. But the structure of its relationship with NOW made it impossible for the LDEF to protect itself from spillover of conflict from NOW because so many leaders held joint positions in both organizations. As an original member in NOW, Tully had chosen to back the Womansurge faction of NOW board members, and this cast the LDEF as partisan in the fight:

There were people who felt that the president of the [LDEF] had no business being involved but nobody sat on me and told me I couldn't do it. So I went ahead and did. . . . All along I was on the other side from the Majority Caucus. . . . That was part of the reason for some friction between NOW and [the LDEF]. (Tully 1992, 112)

Her choice to oppose the more powerful faction in NOW created a rift between the two organizations. Given their subordinate and peripheral status, LDEF leaders could not protect their organization from the problems erupting in NOW.

But there is a second fascinating outcome that emerged from the intertwined relationship between the two groups. During this period of NOW factionalism on the board of directors, the LDEF became a kind of haven for refugees from NOW, tired of the fighting and needing an organizational home (M. Fox, telephone interview with the author, June 1, 2009). While the conflict had created tension between the two groups, Tully (1992, 83, 122) also described the situation as a boon to the LDEF in that it pulled so many competent leaders into the spin-off organization:

I quite deliberately created a little sanctuary in the Legal Defense Fund . . . making it possible for people who didn't want to be bothered with the politics in NOW to stay working at the national level. . . . There was this little oasis, a place where they could go and get away from all the nonsense. I'm sure there was resentment about that. [The split in NOW] pushed some very good people out of the leadership of NOW, and it worked very much to the benefit of the Legal Defense Fund, because I don't know if I would ever have had people of the caliber of Muriel [Fox] and Marilyn Patel and Gene Boyer and Bonnie Howard on the Fund board otherwise. I think they might have seen the Fund as an unimportant sideshow, if it hadn't been for the fact that they didn't want to be involved in all those fights.

NOW leaders repelled by the factionalism on NOW's board were able to find a safe harbor in the LDEF. The structural overlap between NOW and the LDEF eased their transition, keeping them connected, but also protected them from the worst of the conflict until the fighting had resolved. Others left NOW permanently but stayed in the LDEF "oasis" for the rest of their feminist careers.

The transfer of personnel also seemed to protect the LDEF from any retaliatory action that the NOW board might have wanted to take against it for supporting the losing Womansurge faction. Mary Jean Tully, when asked about NOW's control or lack of control over the LDEF, argued that during her tenure at the LDEF, the NOW board had felt frustrated "that they didn't have more control over the Legal Defense and Education Fund" because it was "an offshoot of NOW." But so many founders and important NOW leaders had transferred to the LDEF after the split in the NOW board that they provided a buffer against NOW's interference. The LDEF was "beefed up with a lot of people who had pretty good records in NOW . . . making it safe from attack; they didn't want to lose those people" (Tully 1992, 140). Over time, this exchange of leaders between NOW and the LDEF helped ease the relationship between the two groups. Gene Boyer, a longtime activist in both NOW and the LDEF, confirmed this relationship: "we had this tradition: after you're through being a top-dog in NOW, then you go on to the LDEF" (Boyer 1991, 104).

The serious rift between the two organizations was also healed by their common focus on the ERA. About the campaign, Muriel Fox (2009) remembers:

> NOW LDEF worked very hard. We really shot our entire treasury and everything to get the ERA passed. And do whatever we could within our 501(c)(3) restrictions. We worked very very hard for the ERA and we worked very closely with NOW. I think it was probably working for the ERA that brought us closer together, too.

Over the years, the two organizations have worked together far more often than they have been at odds. But their core–peripheral interdependence creates a constant threat that the problems of one organization will flood into the other, usually in the direction of the LDEF.

While NOW and the LDEF moved past the most threatening conflicts that jeopardized their partnership, it is clear that other problems were intractable, continuing to plague the relationship. Because the LDEF shared a name with NOW, the two organizations continued to be confused with each other in media reports into the 1990s and 2000s. Their tangled status meant that "the media kept getting it wrong and they almost never got it right. [Instead of the LDEF,] they would say, 'NOW did this,' or the Legal committee of NOW, or all sorts of things" (Fox 2009). Maureen McFadden, the vice president of communications, noted that the problem was so bad that "no matter how successful we were in getting media coverage, nine out of ten times they got our name wrong" (Schwartz 2009). Moreover, the LDEF had been told that NOW's radical reputation was a continuing drag on its funding opportunities, with major funding institutions telling LDEF leaders that they would be better able to raise money if they were not associated with NOW. Finally, as NOW aged, it faced a growing reputation that it only catered to the needs of older women. The LDEF could solve some of these problems by moving even further away from NOW's core identity by dropping its name.

In 2004, the LDEF's incoming president, Kathy Rogers, proposed changing the LDEF's name to Legal Momentum. Other leaders agreed that "a new . . . more modern name might attract some younger people" (Fox 2009). This choice marked a clear decision to step back from NOW, dropping the name of the parent organization completely. While the NOW board of directors had the power to refuse this request, and many NOW leaders, including Kim Gandy, NOW's president, thought it was a mistake, ultimately NOW allowed the LDEF to create greater distance between the two organizations.

Social Movement Bureaucracies and Their Satellite Organizations

Other movement organizations have experienced similar rifts with their own satellite groups. In 1997, the Sierra Club Legal Defense Fund changed its name to Earthjustice Legal Defense Fund, leaving its connection to Sierra Club in the past. R. Frederic Fisher, chair of the Earthjustice board, explained the choice as necessary to reflect that the group had grown beyond its initial limited role as a fund-raising branch of Sierra Club: "We began small 26 years ago, doing work primarily on behalf of Sierra Club. Now we're widely known as the 'law firm for the environment' because we serve the entire environmental community on a wide range of concerns" (Earthjustice 1997).

Originally, the Sierra Club Legal Defense Fund was founded because, as with NOW, club leaders understood legal action to be a vital part of attaining its goals, and by creating a separate organization, they would be able to raise tax-deductible money to do it. When the relationship worked well, it was because leaders of both the club and the fund overlapped in their roles and were good friends. Over time, the original overlapping leaders of the fund were replaced by those who had never been in the club's membership and who viewed the parent organization as a competitor. One of these new leaders "wanted the Fund to be run as a separate organization that could go its own way" and, as a part of that effort, established a separate membership base for the fund and hired a separate lobbyist to work for just the fund (McCloskey 2005, 155).

As with NOW and its LDEF, when Sierra Club and its Legal Defense Fund shared a name but were operating as separate organizations, it resulted in "considerable confusion" about who represented Sierra Club in the media, among lawmakers and the public. The two organizations clashed over fund-raising responsibilities, use of the Sierra Club name, and who made decisions about what cases Sierra Club should take on. In the end, the conflicts were irresolvable. When the Sierra Club Legal Defense Fund changed its name to Earthjustice, it severed formal ties with Sierra Club completely. In response, Sierra Club opted to form "its own legal arm within its structure," and according to Michael McCloskey, former executive director of the Sierra Club, both organizations were relieved to be released from the contentious relationship (McCloskey 2005, 156).

In contrast to this rather serious schism between Sierra Club and its satellite organization, NOW did not sever ties with Legal Momentum when it changed its name, and the name change appears not to have signaled any serious decline in their relationship. In part, this is because the relationship itself carries less weight than it did in the past, allowing for lower stakes in negotiating their responsibilities to each other. NOW has created an entire ecosystem of organizations, meaning the LDEF is not its only source of tax-exempt donations. In fact, Fox (2009) remembers that some NOW leaders remarked the name change might mean that NOW could raise more money through its NOW Foundation. This preference for money through the NOW Foundation is a rational calculation for the organization's leaders. While the LDEF (now Legal Momentum) was created with a distinct identity, the other tax-exempt organizations in NOW's ecosystem were created to be much more aligned with NOW's identity. The NOW Foundation, like the LDEF, is a 501(c)(3) and is "devoted to achieving full equality for women through education and litigation" (National Organization for Women Foundation 2017). And like the LDEF, the foundation was designed to bring money to support NOW's work. But while it is also a legally distinct organization, the NOW Foundation was structured so that its interests never diverge from the membership organization. The president of NOW is also the president of the foundation, and the boards of directors directly overlap. According to Maryann Barakso (2004, 127), because of its "educational purposes," the foundation pays for NOW officers to travel around the country giving speeches and presentations. Whereas the most serious problems in the relationship between NOW and its LDEF were caused by the spin-off's need to establish a separate identity, there is no such gap between NOW and its foundation. The foundation exists within NOW's core, making its relationship with NOW leaders seamless in a way that the peripheralized LDEF could never achieve.

This is not to say that creating the educational foundation has not caused any trouble in NOW. Rank-and-file members have sometimes raised questions about whether NOW officers are still accountable to the membership if some of what those leaders do is paid for with foundation dollars rather than through dues. Other complaints focus on how NOW leaders choose national campaigns for the foundation and whether these are driven by funding agencies rather than priorities NOW members care about. As Barakso (2004, 128) notes, members have no voting power in the foundation, yet the foundation and the way it raises money shape NOW's priorities. Any conflict over the foundation arises internally because there is so little space between its identity and priorities and NOW. Perhaps at some point, this internal dissension around the foundation could boil into factionalism. The findings in this book suggest that this kind of conflict is most likely to emerge at the grass roots of the organization.

The closeness between NOW and its educational foundation is not a given; other movement organizations have created similar foundations only to see them develop autonomy from the parent and ultimately rupture the relationship. Sierra Club, again, is instructive as an example of this possibility. In his biographical account of his years as a Sierra Club leader, Michael McCloskey paints a picture of bitter competition between leaders of the club and of its educational foundation over who was "top dog" in their relationship. The foundation, according to McCloskey, saw the membership organization "as being in the hands of undependable people" who were "reckless with money." When he "meekly" approached the foundation for financial help, he felt required to "sing for [his] supper" (McCloskey 2005, 150). The relationship was so bad in the late 1970s that the membership club set up yet another 501(c)(3) organization with the same capabilities as the existing educational foundation but that was directly controlled by members of Sierra Club's executive committee, just as NOW's Foundation is controlled directly by NOW leaders.

NOW's PACs are also intended to match the membership organization's identity with little distinction beyond their tax status. NOW PACs operate at both the national and state levels to legally engage in electioneering for feminist candidates, an activity that NOW itself is forbidden from doing to maintain its status as a 501(c)(4) IRS designation. In the eyes of the IRS, PACs are considered to be "separate tax-exempt entities," but from the outset, NOW's PAC manuals make it clear that the PACs are distinct in name only (National Organization for Women Records 1984). NOW leaders explained to the members that they should think of the PACs as "committee[s] of NOW" rather than separate organizations. In the 1979 manual, leaders explained that structuring the PACs with "over-lapping officers will eliminate potential conflict and retain control within the membership organization. Disagreement between the two bodies saps the energies of activists who are needed in the struggle for feminist goals" (National Organization for Women Records 1979b, 5).

To assure this alignment, NOW insisted that state NOW officers should also be the officers of the state PAC (National Organization for Women Records 1979c, 36). In the PAC manuals, NOW leaders explained to members that by mandating that the officers of NOW also be the officers of the PAC, they would "ensure that the PAC [would] not develop into a separate organization which could be at odds with the membership organization" (National Organization for Women Records 1979b). Like the NOW Foundation, NOW structured the relationship so that the state PACs would not vary from the priorities of the national PAC and the national PAC would remain tightly coupled to the core of the membership organization.

Of course, the legal environment of the organizations forces some distinction between the PAC and the membership organizations. Although NOW donors are not allowed to claim their donations as tax exemptions, NOW's nonprofit tax status protects it from paying taxes on the money it raises. For good reasons, NOW leaders are anxious about protecting the organization from violating the IRS rules for this status, including the careful monitoring of any electioneering engaged in by units of the membership organization. Repeated in each iteration of NOW's PAC manuals, NOW leaders urged members to be careful in making public statements regarding political candidates:

> It should be clearly noted that the statement on behalf of a candidate is from the Political Action Committee of NOW, rather than from the chapter or state organization. This is important for the protection of the tax-exempt status of the organization. (National Organization for Women Records 1979d, 2; see also National Organization for Women Records 1979b)

But this is also plainly spelled out as a false distinction between the two organizations, meant only to satisfy the IRS requirements. The early manuals make clear that the PACs were formed with a single goal in mind: the ERA. NOW formed its PACs to serve as one more set of tools in service of this goal. With the ERA at the center, the manuals emphasize over and over the importance of coordination and unity, sometimes because of IRS reporting issues but more importantly because there needed to be a coordinated national plan to achieve the ERA, NOW's most pressing goal at the time.

While NOW's relationship with its PACs appears to have drawn little controversy from its members, this is not always the case. Sierra Club, for example, struggled with the decision to form a PAC and then with what to do with it. Sierra Club has a more politically diverse membership than NOW; roughly one-third of their members were registered Republicans in the early 1980s when club leaders were deciding to form the PAC (McCloskey 2005). A PAC's central role is to influence the political process by helping to elect sympathetic officials; but a divided membership makes candidate donation decisions controversial. According to McCloskey, however, there was little competition or conflict between Sierra Club and its PAC, a fact that he attributes to "never [spinning it off] into a separate organization" (McCloskey 2005, 153). As in NOW, the Sierra Club PAC was run by mainly the same core executives that ran the membership organization.

The different pathways of NOW's pragmatic splits demonstrate some interesting patterns. NOW's relationships with its PACs and the NOW Foundation appear to be more buffered from conflict than the LDEF was for several reasons. First, unlike the LDEF (now Legal Momentum), they have less need for an independent identity from NOW. Because they are not raising money from more conservative funding institutions and corporations, they need less autonomy from NOW's sometimes polarizing reputation. Second, they require fewer people to run them because they operate as funding vehicles for specific projects. Unlike the LDEF, the only members of PACs and the Foundation are NOW officers, who set the agenda for both groups. Although there is occasional tension over priorities and how to spend NOW's resources, there is no evidence that the PACs or the NOW Foundation have developed the more serious rifts that occurred between the LDEF and NOW. These patterns are not particular to NOW, as indicated by the comparison to Sierra Club. For pragmatic spin-off organizations, the recipe for avoiding conflict after splitting seems to be never really to split at all.

Conclusion

Dividing from a single structure into multiple groups is just one way for bureaucratic movement groups to formalize their work and make it possible for activists with specific skills to specialize in particular functions. NOW repeatedly split into new organizations to attract new resources.

Academics consider this sort of mundane and pragmatic organizational splitting a matter of routine business for organizations and distinct from the kinds of conflict-driven schisms that receive most of our attention. Yet NOW's experience splitting off peripheral, legally distinct satellite organizations reveals a more complicated and interesting relationship. Conflict is not absent from these relationships; it just appears for different reasons and at a different point in the organizations' trajectory. While internal conflict does not drive the decision to split, it often appears after the split, as both resulting organizations attempt to negotiate a new relationship in which they are tied but separate. NOW's history with these splits, especially in comparison to Sierra Club's, demonstrates how these relationships become conflicted.

First, despite everyone's best intentions for the organizations to work with a singular identity and toward shared goals, the LDEF was constructed to be a peripheral and subordinate organization. Initially, this caused little concern; the LDEF was meant to be a "sideshow" fundraising institution. Problems arose when the LDEF asserted greater autonomy from NOW, with distinct and sometimes conflicting needs. But a more equal relationship was a poor fit for the structural realities of its bylaws, which encoded the LDEF's second-rate status. This same pattern occurred in Sierra Club's relationships with its spin-offs, except its membership organization was often considered the junior partner in its relationships.

Second, once new organizations were formed under the same umbrella, particular leaders selected the new organization because it was a better fit with their education, training, interests, and personalities. These personnel shifts helped cultivate different cultures and different strategies for achieving even shared goals. The differences were exacerbated over time, as new people, without histories or friendships that spanned the organizations, joined the groups. This drift created more tension between the core and peripheral organizations.

Third, the core and peripheral organizations faced different resource pressures and requirements to meet their needs. In NOW, the membership organization needed to maintain its members by pursuing the projects and strategies rank-and-file members found inspiring. In contrast, the LDEF needed to appeal to institutional funders, who preferred conservative approaches to advocacy. Had they been totally structurally distinct organizations, these diverging paths would not have been a problem—as noted earlier, social movements benefit from having multiple organizational repertoires operating simultaneously (Walker, McCarthy, and

Baumgartner 2011; Levitsky 2007). But because NOW's core and peripheral organizations diverged while continuing to share a name, the LDEF chafed at the cost of its association with NOW. In effect, although formed to be united—even indistinguishable, the nature of their work created two very different organizations. Their cultural differences and structural proximity increased the amount of conflict and competition between them.

Outside of the LDEF, NOW's history of spinning off new organizations demonstrates that these outcomes are not inevitable. Perhaps to avoid the problems that had emerged in the relationship with the LDEF, NOW leaders created its PACs and its foundation to fit squarely within its core structure. No external leaders or members directly participate in their functioning, and they are explicitly meant to pursue the goals and electoral outcomes desired by national NOW leaders. Although this approach has not made the PACs and the foundation immune to conflict, it does seem to have protected them from a sometimes discordant relationship between NOW's core and the LDEF. Sierra Club, too, seemed to learn this lesson in creating spin-offs; it has shifted to effectively keeping them in-house, with the same leadership as its membership organization.

NOW's system of organizations, and particularly its experience with the LDEF, reveals something fundamentally important about how the regulatory environment shapes bureaucratic movement organizations as well as the larger social movement. Bureaucratic organizations are more vulnerable to this kind of splitting because they are more disposed structurally and culturally to engage in a stratified division of labor. Smaller groups and collectives lack the capacity to create and manage spin-offs, and so this kind of schism is largely limited to formalized bureaucracies like NOW.

As a final note, though bureaucratic organizations are capable and tempted to split in these ways, they also sometimes rethink this strategy. Over time, Sierra Club "changed its mind about the value of spinning off organizations to undertake specialized functions." McCloskey (2005, 156) notes that for the efficiency that comes with specialization, spinning off new organizations often creates more conflicts among unified activists than it solves. NOW has not created any new spin-off organizations since the 1980s.

Schisms Aren't Always Bad

Up to this point, I have focused on the ways bureaucratic structures breed organizational splits. NOW's story, stretched over five decades, demonstrates how bureaucracies can both provide stable infrastructure and serve as important sites of innovation, creativity, and generative conflict for their movements. The same issues that roiled the smaller feminist collectives also created factions within NOW's boundaries, as its decentralized bureaucracy created space for multiple styles of feminism to develop in its peripheral spaces. As this structure provided durable stability, it also planted seeds of organizational schism and groups of members frequently broke away to form new independent groups. In this conclusion, I review how this happened in NOW before turning to the consequences of organizational splits. As we will see, although organizational splits may be inevitable, they need not be inherently destructive. In fact, infighting, factionalism, and schism, however painful in the moment, can be a boon to the resulting organizations and the broader movements they continue to share.

I have discussed a wide range of organizational splits, originating in various places within NOW's structure. By examining the basic model of the bureaucratic core and periphery, we can see how these cases fit together and complete the story of how factions emerge and decide to split away. The model is based on the bureaucratic layering in which members are divided into local, state, and regional levels, and arranged from the organizational periphery in to the core. By dividing large memberships into core and peripheral parts of the organization, decentralized bureaucracies create disparate conditions within the broader structure. When factionalism breaks out in the core areas of the organization, partisans

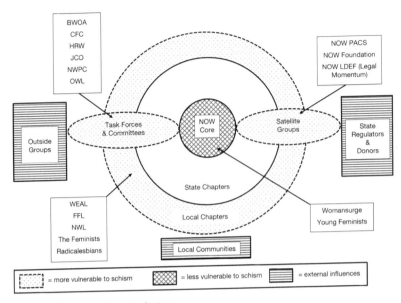

Patterns of organizational splitting.

have clear and significant advantages in waging their fights. Their location at the core of the organization means they have personal relationships with other national leaders, routine access to structural power at national meetings of the board of directors, and structural mobility to move their fight to new parts of the organization, such as the regional and state levels. These benefits were apparent in both Womansurge and the Young Feminist factions as they continued to fight for their priorities in NOW after losing important battles. Both factions used their prominence as national leaders to curry support from rank-and-file members at the state and local levels. When their priorities were denied by the board of directors, they took advantage of their structural mobility to continue their fights in the organizational periphery. At the same time as their proximity to the core provided advantages, it also bound these factions more tightly to NOW's central identity and rules. In this sense, their greater structural power, acquired through their location as national factions, reduced their ability to develop an independent and particular faction identity that might have helped them break away. For factions operating in bureaucratic structures like NOW's, greater power to get what you want comes at the cost of independence and autonomy.

This balance of freedom and power also holds for factions emerging in the bureaucratic periphery. Peripheral factions have greater autonomy to evolve in new directions but little structural power to effect change in the rest of the organization or to move their challenge to different levels. Each peripheral location operates a bit differently, with distinct opportunities and constraints in how factions develop and different external communities that pull them from NOW's core. At the chapter level, members have considerable freedom to make their local groups whatever they want them to be, including latitude to play with the basic power structures and ideologies pressed by the national organization. This dynamic was apparent in a number of schism organizations emerging from local chapters, including the Women's Equity Action League, Feminists for Life (FFL), and National Women's Liberation (NWL).

Similarly, task force and committee members have space to organize in distinct ways, focus their energy how they want, and interact with actors in the environment. The environmental influences are most commonly the state regulators, major donors, outside groups and movements, and the local communities in which factions reside. In this space, new ideologies and values seep into peripheral factions, drawing them further from the bureaucratic core and into closer alignment with the external communities with which they partner. Pressure to break away comes from the increasing space between the organizational core and the peripheralized faction, with the accompanying frustration of operating in the organizational wings. Through this pathway, NOW's task forces and local chapters contributed a variety of new organizations to the feminist movement, including National Women's Liberation, WEAL, the National Women's Political Caucus (NWPC), Catholics for Choice (CFC), and the Older Women's League.

Satellite organizations, like the NOW Legal Defense and Education Fund (LDEF; later renamed Legal Momentum), also develop in conjunction with environmental forces outside of the organization. Satellite organizations are founded with the express intent of managing external relationships with state regulators, election officials, and major donors. Satellite organizations can exist so far out in the periphery that they develop serious rifts with the organization's core. This pattern is apparent in a variety of social movement organizations and their 501(c)(3) satellite groups, including NOW, Sierra Club, and the NAACP. Perhaps in response to the problems that emerged in its relationship with its LDEF, NOW has adopted a different strategy with its political action committees and its foundation; by creating overlapping leadership structures with the NOW membership organization, these satellite groups are folded in much more closely to the bureaucratic core. This virtually immunizes these satellite groups from drifting away, as did the LDEF. In general, the further a membership cluster exists in the periphery, the more dependent it will be on connections and resources in the surrounding environment (Hillman, Withers, and Collins 2009). To the extent that these external communities are significantly different than the organization's core, the greater the pressure will be on the peripheral cluster to factionalize and split away.

There are important moderating factors, both internal and external to the organization, affecting these basic relationships. On the external side, organizations' fortunes are shaped by the levels of public support for their movements. In times of broad movement growth, organizations get a boom in membership and resources. Under these circumstances, there is more space for factions to grow and less pressure to reconcile differences with core leaders. The evidence suggests that most of NOW's splits occurred during the 1970s in no small part because the possibilities for feminist activism seemed limitless. Why engage in lengthy internal organizational battles when there are plenty of potential members and supporters joining the movement? Factions had every reason to believe they would fare well on their own in a context of broad enthusiasm for the movement and plenty of material support for feminist goals.

When the broader movement is ebbing, however, there is greater pressure to consolidate resources, and factions likely weigh the choice to break away more carefully. For the feminist movement, the 1980s brought a lost Equal Rights Amendment (ERA) campaign, the election of Ronald Reagan, and a cultural backlash to feminism, all of which tempered many activists' enthusiasm for starting new organizations. Gene Boyer (1991: 223-224), in her oral history of NOW, lamented that the feminist movement, once thriving with creativity and entrepreneurship, had contracted in the much less promising cultural and political environment. Speaking in 1991, she noted:

> We're losing a lot of organizations. We're getting more consolidation. People are becoming economical and conservative in the use of resources. . . . What started as a single spore and became this big nucleus full of stuff, is going the other way.

It is a reasonable assumption that these same factors dampened many of NOW factions' expectations that they would be able to survive as independent organizations if they broke away, and so many just stayed put or dropped out of the movement completely. As feminists saw declines in the number of organizations, financial support, and even women claiming a feminist identity, faction members had good reason to doubt their ability to survive on their own as independent organizations, and internal conflicts were less likely to spill into a full schism. For the last several decades, the feminist movement, particularly the formalized bureaucratic branch, had no choice but to consolidate as much as possible and weather the constant assertions that it was irrelevant, if not already dead. In these circumstances, the prudent choice for factionalized members is to stay within the parent organization, even if marginalized.

Internally, the circumstances of particular membership clusters can vary independently of how hostile or inviting the external environment may be. Within an organization, new issues can come into vogue, drawing more organizational resources and attention for those leaders and members working on them. Organizations' limited resources create a zero-sum game; as new issues ascend, they press other issues out of the spotlight. This pattern is clear in NOW's treatment of the ERA in the 1970s. Not only were the specific ERA issue committees lavished with attention and resources but NOW's board of directors also mandated that all other committees tie their issues to the ERA. Under these conditions, members who cared deeply about the demoted issues were more likely to strike out on their own. While NOW continues to claim the ERA passage as a goal, it has shifted to prioritize other issues, including issues of racial inequality, intersectional feminism, and anti–sexual assault campaigns. In this way, particular issues can cycle in and out of an organizational core, with greater risk of splitting when they have lost the organizational spotlight.

The Upside of Schism

Organizational splitting in social movements, especially factionalism and schism, has been generally understood to be a destructive event, often fatal for the group itself. In his oft-quoted study of social movement outcomes, William A. Gamson (1990) acknowledges that conflict abounds in organizational life—a misery that deserves its "sorry reputation" (101). He sees formal schism as proof of an organization's inability to manage internal conflict. The price for this failure is heavy, including the group's dramatically reduced ability to achieve any of its goals. According to Gamson, this may be because groups that schism are inherently moribund, and the conflict is merely a symptom of a deeper, fatal disease. Either as a cause or a consequence, splitting spells doom for organization.

Even among those who take a more positive view of conflict's role in movements, splitting apart is viewed as proof of organizational damage.

Amin Ghaziani (2008, 20), for example, draws a line between healthy in-fighting and schism. Infighting, he argues, allows groups to grapple in tangible ways with differences in strategy and identity before "converg[ing] on shared meanings of political organizing." But schism, or group defections, according to Ghaziani, is evidence that organizations have not gleaned the benefits of infighting and instead tipped into failure. When groups of members break away to establish a new group, they deprive the original organization of their energy, skill, and dedication (Gamson 1990; Hirschman 1970). Across the literature, it is generally taken as self-evident that schism is a death sentence.

While factionalism and splitting can be quite painful for the people and groups involved, there is good reason to be more optimistic about how activist communities, both in specific organizations and in the broader movements, might actually benefit from organizational splitting. By and large, splitting is a gradual process, the result of pressures that build over time as the principal actors begin to recognize that the path to what they want may lead outside the organization. As many of the cases discussed in previous chapters demonstrate, most of the groups that broke away from NOW continued to recognize the benefits of NOW's presence and influence in the movement. They did not want NOW to be torn apart; they just wanted to express an approach to feminism that was less feasible from within NOW's boundaries. Factions grew tired of fighting to make NOW what it could not or did not want to be. Sometimes this led to hard feelings in the moment, but overwhelmingly, after the splits, the breakaway organizations continued to collaborate with NOW.

The very breadth of issues that were represented by these factions demonstrates why splitting is sometimes necessary. NOW simply could not be everything to everyone—Gainesville members wanted more direct action and a grassroots orientation; the women who formed the Older Women's League wanted to bring more attention and tangible services devoted to older women; the Women's Equity Action League (WEAL) left to create a safer place for more conservative women and to avoid controversial social issues like abortion; and The Feminists left to create more space for radical feminism. Rather than continuing to hit a brick wall trying to change NOW, these factions broke away to channel their time and energy exactly as they wished into the styles of activism and the issues that compelled them most.

That factions benefit from breaking away is easily understood—after all, it is these subgroups making the active, hopeful choice to start over. Yet splitting can also be a net positive event for the original parent organization. In the short run at least, following a split, the parent organization gets a reprieve from internal conflict. While the most extreme forms of factionalism—those dramatic episodes that claim most of our attention—are capable of destroying an organization, most conflicts involve small groups splitting away without really endangering the parent organization. When the conflict is more serious, a schism of some members may usher in a period of peace and solidarity, with members focusing on the goals, strategies, and targets that unite them rather than wrangling over what divides them. In this way, as Balser notes, a schism can actually help an organization survive longer than if factions had stayed and fought (Balser 1997; Coser 1956).

Splitting can bring relief to the parent organization in other ways as well. After Elizabeth Farians stepped down from NOW's Task Force on Women in Religion and the New York members broke away to form CFC, both sides found the new arrangement far more beneficial than the old. Catholic feminists had struggled to gain traction with the Catholic Church when they were working as NOW members, and most NOW leaders had little interest in devoting energy and resources to reforming religious institutions. Splitting into distinct organizations allowed both organizations to do the work they were best suited to do. Importantly, after CFC was formed, the two organizations maintained a congenial relationship, sharing members and leaders and working together on a host of projects. Frances Kissling (telephone interview with the author, April 23, 2009), a former leader of CFC, describes the relationship with NOW as cooperative and convenient:

> The relationship between Catholics for Choice and NOW has always been a very positive relationship. I don't think there has been a period in the organizational history that NOW was not happy that [CFC] existed. . . . In some ways you could say that [CFC] was instrumentalized, you know? "We've got our Catholics we can pull out when we need to counter the Bishops." [CFC] has always been its own organization, but it's always been seen by the movement as . . . you know, we've got to have somebody Catholic to counter these Catholic Bishops. We can't be standing up as feminists who are barely religious, talking about Catholics. So, it's great to have these women who could do it.

As separate organizations, CFC was better able to assert an authentic Catholic identity and NOW was able to rely on a broadened feminist community to do some of the work for which it was less equipped.

Although parent organizations may get some reprieve from conflict following a split, it's worth noting that the contentious issues that precipitated the split do not automatically disappear when a faction leaves. Factions may leave behind some supporters who, uncertain about starting over in a new organization, will continue to push for those same priorities or strategies, and others may participate in forming the new group while continuing their membership in NOW. An illustrative example of just this process followed the purge of NOW lesbians from the New York chapter in the 1970s. While some of the lesbians who were pushed out by Betty Friedan formed schism groups like Radicalesbians, others stayed, continuing the fight to make NOW a more just organization for LGBTQ members. At the Second Congress to Unite Women, in New York City in 1970, a group of lesbians interrupted the speeches to protest the way they had been maligned as a threat to NOW and to the movement. Martha Shelley, a member of Radicalesbians and a continuing member of NOW, recalled the action's impact: "That was when NOW really started taking the lesbian issue seriously" (Shelley 2003).

In fact, largely because so many lesbians remained in NOW to continue pressuring the organization to consider their needs, lesbian rights continued to occupy a place in NOW's internal politics. As Gilmore and Kaminski (2007) note, many lesbians lived in places where a local chapter of NOW was the only option for a feminist organization. Others stayed because of misogyny in the gay liberation movement. Even at those times during which NOW remained indifferent or hostile to lesbians' rights, some of these women continued to fight within NOW for recognition and support. This rank-and-file effort at the local, state, and regional levels culminated in a national conference vote in 1971 to officially include lesbian rights as a core part of NOW. In 1973, national NOW formally established a task force devoted to sexuality and lesbianism, and a broad coalition of members continued to work for lesbian rights inside and outside of NOW for many years thereafter (Pomerleau 2010).

New organizations that form as the result of a split also benefit in important ways from their origination in a parent organization like NOW. Of course, painful conflict is not a happy way to begin life as a new organization. But leaders in these schisms sometimes spent years cultivating organizational skills and connections that benefited their new organizations. When Aileen Hernandez, Eleanor Spikes, and Patsy Fulcher founded Black Women Organized for Action (BWOA), they had already worked together for years as leaders at the national level of NOW and in chairing NOW's National Task Force on Minority Women and Women's

Rights. These experiences undoubtedly helped shape their ideas of what BWOA would be. Kimberly Springer (2005) argues that of all the black women's organizations she included in her book, BWOA maintained the tightest ties to the mainstream, largely white feminist movement, in large part because of these founders' experiences in NOW.

Yet while BWOA's founders emulated many aspects of NOW in their initial organizational efforts, their experiences in NOW also helped them clarify what they did not want in their new organization—most notably, they learned that taking on too many issues could distract from a primary focus on black women's experiences and leadership. They also rejected a centralized, national leadership structure in favor of a locally focused organization with rotating chairs (Springer 2005).

Similarly, when the founders of WEAL were organizing, they were able to capitalize on their members' common understanding of what a feminist organization could look like because many of them had already been organized into NOW's chapter structure. Leaders could use a shorthand reference for their new group—a "conservative NOW"—to bypass some of the identity work they would otherwise have had to do (Costain and Costain 1987). The phrase quickly communicated a critical message: we are doing what we did before, but in a less controversial way. For both groups, the benefits of this split, while perhaps not immediately obvious to all NOW leaders, became clear in the ensuing years—NOW faced less pressure to represent the more restrained version of feminism that was preferred by the women who exited for WEAL, and WEAL was able to represent a toned-down feminism for women who were uncomfortable with NOW.

Beyond helping the specific groups that are involved in a schism, splits can also nourish the broader movement in which these groups exist. NOW's propensity to split off groups of members into new organizations provided the feminist movement with many more places for nascent feminists to plug in, especially at times and places where NOW felt like the only option. Scholars have long recognized the challenges that generalist organizations face in cultivating clear roles in their movements (Stryker 2000; Carroll and Swaminathan 2000). People respond in deeply personal ways to organizational styles and structures, and activists create and choose structures that reflect their sense of how the world should be. Sarah Soule and Brayden King (2008) argue that generalist organizations, which tend to be larger and more bureaucratic than most other groups, struggle to attract members and supporters who are predisposed to disliking that particular style of organizing, even when the group is working on the issues they care about. Because some people will always prefer smaller, specialist organizations that feel more personal, the generalist organization's large bureaucratic structure and broad set of priorities will prevent some people from joining. Disputes over the meaning of organizational structure play out in most social movements, and American feminism is one of the most studied cases of these disputes and their consequences.

Yet structure and style preferences are not the only dynamics at play when organizations split apart. Issue strategies and cultural orientation play critical roles as well. When Patricia Goltz and Cathy Callahan started FFL, they supported the vast majority of NOW's agenda, quibbling only over its support for abortion rights, which they believed was keeping lots of feminists away from NOW. And in Columbus, Ohio, where FFL had its start, there were few other options for feminist activism. By splitting off a new organization, Goltz and Callahan wanted to diversify the movement's approach to reproductive rights (Kretschmer 2014). Though FFL has since grown far more aligned with the conservative religious pro-life movement, in its first years, it strove to provide an organizational bridge for its members, who were aligned with mainstream feminist, peace, and anti-abortion movements. They framed this choice as strategic as much as ideological.

This kind of splitting also occurred among the leaders and founders of NOW, who recognized that the organization was limited in its ability to be everything to everyone. In 1968, responding to the divisiveness of abortion rights in NOW, Betty Friedan, along with Larry Lader and Bernard Nathanson, established the National Association for the Repeal of Abortion Laws (NARAL) (which, following the Supreme Court decision *Roe v. Wade* legalizing abortion across the nation, became the National Abortion Rights Actions League) in Chicago. While Friedan pushed NOW to be more active on the abortion rights issue early on, she also knew that there was a place for a single-issue organization dedicated wholly to reproductive rights (Friedan 2000). By creating NARAL, she could be more aggressive on the issue while also providing information to other organizations like NOW. NOW's board minutes for the June 1969 meeting make the assertion that the two groups would cooperate in working toward the repeal of abortion restrictions:

> NARAL, a new group meant to initiate and coordinate repeal activities across the country, was formed at a February repeal conference in Chicago (attended by many NOW activists) and is catching hold in large part because of NOW members' participation in setting its

goals and actions. NARAL will be a key source of information for
NOW chapters as they work to create liaisons with local abortion-
repeal groups for state-level action. (National Organization for
Women Records 1969)

The stable working relationship that NARAL has maintained with NOW
has enabled it to play a more specialized and instrumental role.

This pattern was also apparent when several well-known NOW leaders and founders, including Karen DeCrow and Betty Friedan, participated in the founding of the NWPC, despite the presence of a NOW
task force that was devoted to politics (see chapter 5). Partnering with
Bella Abzug and Gloria Steinem, the cadre of NOW leaders sponsored
and worked on behalf of the new organization. For the NOW leaders,
cutting themselves free from NOW meant fewer restrictions from NOW
members who were not convinced that feminist progress could be made
within the major political parties. It also meant reaching people who
would not have joined NOW in the first place. For Abzug and Steinem,
among others, the NWPC was attractive precisely because it was not a
NOW property. Mary Jean Collins points to this as a major motivating
factor in founding a new, distinct organization, saying that "people didn't
want everything to be in NOW" (M. J. Collins, telephone interview with
the author, May 29, 2009). Although there were strong connections to
NOW, NWPC was intentionally created to attract women who would not
otherwise have been associated with NOW (Cohen 1988). Betty Friedan
(1998, 211) describes the reach of NWPC as "broader than the membership of NOW or of 'women's lib' groups; it would reach some who had
not yet identified themselves as feminist."

Elizabeth Farians tells a similar story when explaining the Joint Committee of Organizations Concerned with the Status of Women in the
Church, a spin-off she formed when she served as the chair of NOW's
Women in Religion task force that was itself a precursor to the breakaway CFC. By forming a new organization, Farians was able to work
with women who would never have joined or worked with NOW, and
the literature they produced makes only cursory mention of NOW. An
explanatory brochure for the new group plants the justification for wom-
en's equality firmly in biblical and Catholic documents from Vatican II,
and the origin story of the group entirely omits Farians's work in NOW,
noting only that she was a "Catholic theologian, who saw the need for
the unification of the efforts which were being made to attain equal status
for women in the Church. The organizations which united together for

action had been working on an individual basis for many years" (Elizabeth Farians Papers 1972).

In reality, as Farians notes, "it was a NOW thing"—Farians conceived of the joint effort as part of her work in NOW even as she recruited outside leaders to be the face of its operation (telephone interview with the author, June 25, 2009). According to Farians, other NOW leaders had no problem with the creation of a new group to focus on the Catholic Church. Just as Kissling describes NOW's relationship with CFC, NOW leaders were only too happy to outsource that work to specialists, leaving them with more resources to focus on other issues, such as employment and reproductive rights.

Although these episodes portray the upsides of splitting and the rosier side of social movement group cooperation following a schism, the picture is incomplete without considering a more sobering, practical reality: to do their work, all groups must compete for the same scarce resources, especially money, members, and media attention. Resource mobilization scholars have explored how this competition affects the ability of movement groups to cooperate with one another. When John McCarthy and Mayer Zald (1977) introduced their theory of resource mobilization, they brought attention to the routine organizational challenges of social movements, noting that even when groups agree generally on goals, they are also competing for the same members, resource streams, media attention, and attention from policy makers. At the same time that they share a common vision for the future, co-movement groups are also competing for advantages that will help them survive.

But this dynamic does not automatically translate into fierce or uncooperative relationships between groups. In fact, the activists included here were all quite clear that while there may have been rough spots in some of the relationships, most of the organizations, even those born in conflicted beginnings, continued to cooperate with one another. Muriel Fox, a founding member of NOW and a longtime leader of both the membership organization and the LDEF (now Legal Momentum), repeatedly asserts that while some splits were contentious because of the personalities involved, the working relationships afterward remained consistently strong and productive. For example, when asked about the splits with the Radicalesbians, Fox (2009) noted:

> Certainly Rita Mae [Brown] and some of those kept referring to NOW people as, you know, club ladies and said they were homophobic, etcetera, like that. So, Rita Mae was always antagonistic, but . . . we

all worked together on certain issues and more and more as the years
went on.

Fox tells a similar story of collaboration with the NWPC, despite a rocky
start because of difficult personalities, noting that "individuals had their
resentments, and Betty Friedan was certainly in the middle of a lot of
that, but there was no conflict at all between NOW and the Caucus. We
certainly worked together." All counted, Fox brought up cooperative relationships between NOW and its breakaway organizations no fewer than
fifteen times in our interview.

Fox is not alone in painting this picture. Other activists, while proud
of the leadership role NOW played and continues to play in the movement, were clear that they did not believe NOW accomplished its goals in
isolation from the groups that broke away. Shelley Fernandez (2009) used
her local NOW consciousness-raising group as a springboard to form a
legally distinct battered women's shelter:

> Casa de las Madres (shelter) came out of NOW. . . . The shelter was
> totally connected to NOW, and all the people involved in it were all
> members of NOW. . . . It was very close [to NOW] because at that
> time, I was president of San Francisco NOW . . . and I was also on the
> national board of NOW. . . . Several of the national board members
> really took it out to their own communities.

Fernandez's account of the founding of the battered women's shelter mir-
rors Stephanie Gilmore's findings in her study of local chapters of NOW
that describe the perforation of NOW's boundaries by members doing
what NOW itself was not structurally equipped to do. In 1974, Memphis
NOW members collaborated with a variety of other feminist groups in
the area to found and staff the Women's Resource Center (WRC), which
focused on securing grants from local and state governments to fund its
service to women suffering from sexual and domestic violence. Gilmore
argues that the creation of the more moderate and institutionally oriented
WRC allowed the NOW chapter to expand its more radical ideologies
and tactics (Gilmore 2013, 58–59). In their survey of feminist organizing in the second half of the twentieth century, Ferree and Hess (2000,
66) similarly argue that when WEAL and NOW split apart, "WEAL's
moderation and emphasis on litigation left NOW free to experiment with
more radical forms of confrontation," including "protests, strikes, and
mass demonstrations."

The benefits of organizational splits are not limited to the feminist movement. Many of the most well-known organizations in the environmental movement have survived despite experiencing splits; many owe their existence to a group of members deciding to strike out on their own to fill a gap in the movement. Friends of the Earth and Greenpeace both emerged from splits within Sierra Club when certain leaders decided that the broader movement needed a different approach. David Brower, founder of Friends of the Earth and a variety of other spin-off organizations, has been clear that even after splitting, the resulting organizations remained connected, linked by their mutual goals for the broader movement. He noted, "I founded Friends of the Earth to make the Sierra Club look reasonable. Then I founded Earth Island Institute to make Friends of the Earth look reasonable" (Postrel 1990).

The feminist movement has been particularly plagued with identity-driven schisms. This sort of splitting is probably less common in other movements, such as the environmentalist movement. But many of the same structural origins of schism are likely to appear across social movements. This is true for both the small collectives and the large, federated, bureaucratic groups. For example, as we have seen in earlier chapters, Sierra Club and NOW faced similar pressures to divide off satellite organizations, and both faced serious factionalism in managing these relationships. And like NOW, Sierra Club has a large network of local chapters, embedded in local environmentalism communities. In these communities, it is reasonable to expect cross-pollinating memberships between local Sierra Club groups and smaller, more radical environmental groups in their area. Under these circumstances, we should expect that these relationships might foster and exacerbate factionalism at the local level of Sierra Club, just as they did for NOW chapters embedded in local feminist communities. Future research could explore how the model of organizational splitting I present here might help us understand the similarities and differences in these processes across a variety of social movements.

As these examples illustrate, even when they are born of conflict, organizational splits do not preclude positive working relationships and collaborations after the groups have separated. In fact, the evidence seems clear that in many cases, splitting can be a functional solution for the need to divide up movement work. In this important alternative vision of how organizational schism affects movement relationships, activists are able to capitalize on multiple streams of ideology and resources to build a robust and durable movement, bound by multiple styles of organizing. Far from being a death knell, the process of moving some functions, projects, ideologies, or strategies outside of the initial group and into new organizational forms can help fill out the movement, creating multiple entry points for activists and securing multiple resource streams in the pursuit of common goals (Disney and Gelb 2000).

This book has taken us one step further in assessing how organizations break apart. It is reasonable to assume that most people, as rational actors, will find a way to work together toward their common goals, even after schisms that nobody initially wanted. But the evidence from NOW suggests that activists also make the decision to split their organizations strategically, with clear eyes about the limitations of what any one organization can achieve on its own.

Many of the organizations that split from NOW created new organizational forms that were meant to correct for the problems that sprang from NOW's decentralized bureaucracy. In other words, they created organizations that did something different from NOW and with a different structure from NOW's. BWOA enacted a team-leadership approach, with three coordinators working together for three-month terms. Leaders could focus on whatever they wanted, and the organization alternated between working with the black power movement, the mainstream feminist movement, and institutional politics. This allowed BWOA leaders to focus on the things they valued as individuals while sharing collaborative responsibility for the direction of the organization. Similarly, when a faction from NOW's Legal Task Force split to form Human Rights for Women (HRW) in 1968 they adopted a consensus decision-making process and a rotating system for leadership among the five directors. They dismissed the idea of creating a membership organization completely (Mary O. Eastwood Papers 1968). Perhaps burned out by the roiling fights in NOW, they opted for a simpler organizational design and a smaller set of goals. HRW worked on the cases it had taken out of NOW, published a job-discrimination handbook, and made small grants to nonprofits and research projects relating to women's employment discrimination (M. Eastwood, telephone interview with the author, June 19, 2009). Even though it was a very different kind of organization, HRW continued to have a relationship with NOW through movement work, including recruiting individual members of NOW also to serve in HRW and partnering with NOW in coalition work on legislation (Mary O. Eastwood Papers 1970a, 1970b).

WEAL, emerging from another very early split in NOW, also considered the benefits to the larger movement of having differently oriented organizations to represent the considerable variety of American women's interests. Founder Betty Boyer wrote to Marguerite Rawalt, chair of NOW's

Legal Committee, that she wanted to avoid NOW's "flamboyant publicity" and that WEAL would work for quiet influence, in contrast to NOW's more abrasive style (Marguerite Rawalt Papers 1968). In an archived letter to a researcher, Bernice Sandler, an early WEAL member, wrote, "[Boyer] set up WEAL so that it dealt only with issues concerning legal and tax inequalities, education, and employment (all broad based issues which are not really controversial)" (Women's Equity Action League Records 1976). WEAL's conservative style reflected the preferences of its founders, but it was also a strategic choice designed to bring more moderate women into the feminist movement. In a letter to Phineas Indritz, a lawyer working in NOW, Boyer highlighted how other movements had benefited from diversity among organizations:

> In forming another, more practical and conservative group, we have
> no intentions of undermining or being publicly critical of NOW. . . .
> If the negro movement can have several groups, of varying militancy
> and temperament, we see no reason why we should not do likewise.
> (Women's Equity Action League Records 1968)

These examples clearly demonstrate how NOW activists often make decisions to branch out on their own in ways meant to supplement and complement NOW's efforts. Some of these spin-offs, like its satellite organizations the LDEF and the NOW political action committees, are utterly strategic splits that meant to work around a regulatory environment. But this sort of strategizing also holds true when there is a long period of conflict leading up to the split, when factional members, who were genuinely trying to transform NOW's operation, came up short in those efforts. When the Gainesville faction finally broke away to form National Women's Liberation after more than a decade of struggle, group leader Candi Churchill (telephone interview with the author, July 6, 2009) noted that she and many of those in the new group would continue to support NOW:

> I'll always be a NOW member. . . . We're all NOW members. . . . We
> believe in it. Like, if you have a union, you join the union. And you
> might have a caucus in your union that is fighting for [something] particular. . . . We've all been NOW members and we will continue to be.

Churchill points to the new group's continued connection to NOW as a critical point of unity, likening it to the solidarity of labor unions. Separating from NOW, even under contentious circumstances, did not dampen the sense of broader unity in sharing a movement.

Even with contentions splits in which no members of the new group retain their ties to the parent organization, activists often see the benefits in hindsight. Jo Freeman, describing the first Congress to Unite Women as a disaster of "backbiting" and "name-calling," argues that even after such a combative event, feminists, especially those in NOW, began to realize that "a diverse movement might be more valuable than a united one." While internal divisions hindered cooperation on joint projects, they ultimately allowed the movement to expand, offering new and creative ways to be feminist that appealed to a broader swath of people. She writes, "As the various feminist groups became more tolerant of one another they also became more cooperative" (Freeman 1975, 228). Although Freeman was referring to divisions between branches of the movement, we can apply the same sort of optimism to the ways organizations split apart. Resultant groups often find a great deal of peace after making the decision to leave, particularly after a split that follows a long, bruising battle. This is true not just because they are able to move forward in the ways that make sense to them but also because a new relationship with their former organization is suddenly possible.

To borrow a framework from Francesa Polletta (2002), an organizational split can lead to something akin to friendship, with the resulting groups able to cooperate outside of the obligations of sharing an organizational structure. Within NOW's structure, members were tied to the decisions of leaders at the top of the organization. By breaking away, faction members were able to let NOW be what it was while they forged a new path that sought to complement rather than compete with NOW. In a relationship reformulated as a friendship, breakaway organizations can "recognize each other's different competencies," with those differences making for a "richer relationship" rather than one that is single-dimensional or unequal (Polletta 2002, 153). In the many interviews I conducted and drew from for this analysis, women who had left NOW to form new groups overwhelmingly and consistently expressed support for NOW's role in the feminist movement. This was true even as they insisted that they could not have reached their goals if they had stayed a part of NOW. They also recognized how the decisions about their new organizations were shaped by their experiences as members of NOW and the value of those experiences, even as they sought to build something different.

I have argued in a variety of different ways that bureaucratic, generalist organizations like NOW are prone to splitting for the very reasons that they are also so stable and durable—they are able to grow large, decentralized, and varied in the projects and collective identities they incubate.

I have also argued that splitting, while sometimes painful to those involved, is inevitable for organizations like this and can produce positive outcomes for the groups and the movements they continue to share.

But for some NOW members, its generalist orientation and broad structure do create uncertainty about what its role should be in the movement. Mary Jean Collins (interview), who served as NOW's first task force coordinator, recalls difficulty explaining to the public why they should support NOW over the groups that were specializing in specific issues:

> If you are everything to everyone, then who are you? And you know, if you've got another group that's formed now that's going to deal with abortion, then what's your role? Then what are you doing? Then what does NOW do about abortion if there is NARAL and Planned Parenthood? What's the unique role of a multi-issue organization? . . . It's a beautiful story in the sense that the children of NOW have made a tremendous contribution. But what does a generalist organization do?

This is a critical question that deserves attention. It is one thing to assert that splitting need not be fatal for groups. But Collins also points to that ever-present issue of resource allocation: groups, even when they are mutually aligned, must compete for the same pool of money, members, and attention; there are simply never enough of these resources to go around. If bureaucratic groups like NOW are spinning off new competitors that are more targeted in their identities and goals, this could cause potential problems for the parent organization.

Of course, survival per se is not NOW's primary mission. As the first and largest feminist organization to kick off the 1960s wave of feminism, NOW remains the dominant organization in the field, with more members, money, and visibility than any other group in the movement. Seen in this light, perhaps it is best to think of NOW not as competing with other organizations but as an incubator of ideas, ideologies, and identities that can replenish the broader feminist movement. NOW chapters can be a place where activists find one another, establish common bonds, decide what's important to them, and then branch off in new directions to pursue new goals. So many of the stories in this book begin in recognition of NOW as a place where activists have come to understand themselves and the world in new ways, before branching out to build something more specific and more personal. As an incubator, NOW can continue to serve this vital role for the larger movement—creating spaces for members to generate new ideas and identities over time before launching some of these members to create new and autonomous spaces of their own.

This is a critical function, too, in a current environment of uncertainty and change, in feminist movements specifically and American politics in general. Not all leaders of NOW are likely to embrace a decentered vision for their organization, and a version of this debate has plagued it for a long time. In her oral history of NOW, Gene Boyer recalls disagreeing with former NOW president Ellie Smeal on the question of how much primacy to give NOW's well-being versus prioritizing the broader movement. Where Smeal was "dead set against coalition building, unless NOW could be the leader and control the coalition," Boyer (1991, 149) argued that NOW's role was to help build a broader women's movement—"to reach out to many kinds of women and many different publics, to embrace them and draw the circle large enough include them, even traditional women, and mainstream women, women in other organizations, women who may never join NOW." These rival visions will shape how individual leaders respond to internal factions and the context for their decision to break away or stay. Leaders embracing a more expansive view of the movement are not likely to fight as hard to keep factions inside; leaders who prioritize their organization's prominence will likely to fight to keep them in. Future research in a variety of organizations and social movements should bear this relationship out.

Conclusion

Much of this book focuses on the 1960s and 1970s, in large part because it was during this time that the feminist movement was rapidly expanding. I write this in the first half of the tumultuous presidency of Donald Trump, whose successful campaign against Hillary Clinton shocked so many on the political left, feminists in particular. In no small measure, his victory was a vicious confirmation of the social acceptability of misogyny and regressive notions of women's value in society. Trump's presidency is a vivid reminder that feminist victories can be incomplete and temporary.

At the same time, the Trump presidency released a tidal wave of feminist mobilizing, both within institutional politics and in the streets—just as political opportunity theorists would predict. In the year following Trump's election, more than twenty-six thousand women contacted Emily's List, a political organization supporting pro-choice female candidates, for information on how to run for political office (Schriok, n.d.). Fourteen thousand women have applied for its training boot camp for running a campaign; fewer than a thousand enrolled in the previous election cycle (Halper 2017). In the fall of 2018, a record number of women were elected to the House of Representatives (Zernike 2018).

Buoyed by online social media forums like Facebook and Twitter, progressive groups overwhelmed the U.S. Capitol switchboard to express opposition to Neil Gorsuch, Trump's nominee for the Supreme Court (Mascaro 2017). This mobilization strengthened Democratic senators' resolve to filibuster his nomination and forced Senate Republicans to make a costly adjustment to Senate rules to get around them. In 2017, activists organized a wide variety of demonstrations, including a women's strike (Stein, Chandler, and Somashekhar 2017), a march for science, a climate march (protesting the new administration's promised rollbacks to environmental protections) (Mooney, Heim, and Dennis 2017), a march for truth (arguing for an investigation into Trump's campaign connections to Russian efforts to influence the 2016 presidential election) (Stein 2017), and protests against Brett Kavanaugh's appointment to the Supreme Court (Witt 2018). Although Washington, D.C., generally sees a high number of protest events, even during less contentious times, the National Park Service saw a 25 percent increase in requests for permits to protest from the previous year (Stein 2017). When Republicans controlled all three branches of the federal government, progressive mobilization made it difficult for Congress to pass legislation for budgets, health care, immigration, and tax reform.

This sense of urgency has also reinvigorated feminist organizing. Following Trump's election, feminists were the first to jump into the protesting fray, with the Women's March. Despite the fractious dissent around the event, by any measure, it was massively successful, mobilizing between 3.3 million and 4.6 million people across the United States, making it the largest protest event in the nation's history (Waddell 2017; Friedersdorf 2017). In Washington, D.C., alone, the roughly five hundred thousand participants in the Women's March dwarfed the inauguration crowd from the day before by a factor of 3.

On the Wednesday morning following the election, NOW's website crashed, unable to handle the wave of traffic it received from people concerned about what a Trump presidency would mean for women's rights (Bayless 2016). In an email exchange with me about NOW's growth following Trump's election (M. E. Ficarra, pers. comm., June 21, 2017), NOW's press coordinator confirmed that the organization has seen its membership climb in 2017, with dozens of new requests to form local

NOW chapters. The closing months of the year also brought the mobilization of feminists against sexual harassment and assault, in the form of the #MeToo movement, first initiated by Tarana Burke (Garcia 2017). Millions of women, most of whom were not members of any formal feminist organization, posted to social media sites about their own stories of sexual harassment and coercion with the hashtag #MeToo. A second watershed moment arrived when dozens of high-profile men in entertainment, news media, and politics were exposed for sexual misconduct, harassment, and assault. The stories were often referred to as "open secrets," meaning many people had known about them, but the men never seemed to face any consequences for the predatory behavior. In 2017, these accusations were met with a new sense of outrage and mobilization to oust perpetrators from their powerful positions.

And on the one-year anniversary of the historic first Women's March, women and men again filled the streets across American cities, with crowds nearly as large as the first (Chira 2018). It is worth noting that many of the Women's Marches held in 2018 were planned and organized by new and revitalized local NOW chapters.

The surge in feminist consciousness is promising for the movement; it is also fractured along the same lines that have divided feminists for decades. Women's March organizers have been deluged with criticism for whitewashing the feminist response to the conservative political climate. The national leaders adjusted their approach, expanding and diversifying the organizing team and seeking help from more seasoned national organizations. These adjustments did not stem the discussion of intersectional feminism, and in many ways, these organizational changes put these issues at the forefront of every local march.

We can see how these fights have already reshaped NOW's agenda. In March 2017, NOW launched a new National Action Program to help chapters and members address a mix of new and established issues. The regular, standby causes were there—the ratification of the ERA and the advancement of reproductive justice, to name just two—but so too are a variety of new issues that reflect an evolving sense of what the organization is and who it should represent, including programs on the "sex-abuse-to-prison pipeline," immigrant rights, and voting rights (National Organization for Women 2017). By 2018, in response to the #MeToo movement, NOW formed a coalition of feminist organizations to hold the Enough Is Enough Summit, an effort to prioritize issues of sexual assault and harassment, with a particular focus on how these problems impact "women of color, low-income women, and LGBTQIA+ women" (National Organization for Women 2018).

These are welcome additions to the NOW agenda and are likely to be embraced by members just joining the organization who come from activist communities devoted to the intersections of race, class, sexuality, and gender. At the same time, given NOW's history and the trajectory of American feminist movements, we can expect many of the same patterns that I detailed throughout this book to play out again in this new wave of growth and expanding agendas. As feminist movements begin to see rising enthusiasm and an upswing in support, there will be less pressure to batten down the organizational hatches. Instead, small groups of members may once again grow frustrated by the limitations of organizational compromises and see promise in breaking out on their own. They may form a broad swath of new organizations, structured and focused in ways that reflect their own specific sensibilities. In fact, I expect that we will see an increase in the rate of splits occurring in NOW and other established feminist organizations as their ranks swell with new activists. As should be made clear by the foregoing chapters, I do not think of this as a bad thing; rather, it can very well signal movement success, hopefulness, and expansion. Most of these breakaway organizations will collaborate when and where it makes sense to join forces. Where such collaborations are less promising, they will split apart to focus on the more narrowly defined projects that motivate their members.

As NOW members and leaders struggle to capitalize on the new political momentum, some internal relationships may grow contentious. Yet it remains unclear how these fights and internal struggles will shape the movement as it surges forward. In this book, I have argued that no organizational form offers the one magic bullet that will meet all activists' needs. Even those organizational forms that offer the greatest stability and the greatest protection against environmental uncertainty—decentralized bureaucracies—cannot meet all needs equally. Some members in these groups will schism and generate new organizational vehicles to meet their niche interests. In this way, even as organizational boundaries narrow, movement boundaries expand.

Data Sources and Research Methods

Data and Analysis Overview

The origin of this project lies in an earlier study. While conducting a case comparison of two organizations that claimed a feminist ideology while taking opposing positions on abortion, I discovered both were founded within a few years of each other in Ohio as local splinters of the National Organization for Women (NOW) (Kretschmer 2009). This sparked a deeper investigation into how NOW, and organizations like it, experience factionalism and schism. In this direction, the current project developed in a three-step process.

First, I used a variety of academic studies, histories, journalistic accounts, memoirs, and biographies to locate cases of factionalism and organizational splitting in NOW. To cast a wide net, I included any mention of an organizational founder's prior membership in NOW, any examples of NOW's intentional founding or seeding of a new organization, and any reference to factionalism within NOW, regardless of whether it resulted in a schism. Second, for each case on the resulting list, I searched again for academic studies, histories, journalistic accounts, memoirs, and biographies specific to its development or its founders. I paid particular attention to those sources that conveyed information about its founding circumstances and principal activists. Third, I collected data about NOW and its organizational offshoots from archives and interviews with members. I deal with each of these data sources separately in the following pages.

All documents and interview transcripts were organized, coded, and analyzed using AtlasTi, a qualitative software program. Following in the example of similar organizational studies (King 2008), I employed a modified grounded theory approach (Glaser and Strauss [1967] 2017). I examined interviews and documents for themes in how and where conflicts emerged among members and leaders. This included taking note of important issues, debates, events, participants, and trajectories of conflicts through the contemporaneous documents and the recollections afterward.

Interview Sources

My data set included forty-five interviews (with forty-two activists) from four sources. The first set consisted of fourteen semistructured original interviews I conducted in 2009 and 2010 with activists who had been NOW leaders and/or breakaway leaders between 1966 and 2009. Interview length ranged from thirty minutes to two hours. Each interview was recorded and transcribed according to the informed consent agreement with the subjects.

The second set of interviews from which I draw are from the Tully–Crenshaw Feminist Oral History Project at the Harvard University Schlesinger Library. These oral history interviews were conducted between 1980 and 1997 with past NOW leaders. They were asked about their personal biographies, their participation in and contributions to the women's movement, and NOW's organizational history. From the overall set, I focus on eighteen interviews with activists who spoke directly about cases of conflict, factionalism, and organizational splitting.

The third set of interviews comes from the Voices of Feminism Oral History Project in the Sophia Smith Collection at Smith College. This project included activists engaged across a variety of American social movements and included topics covering their childhood, personal life, and political work. From this project, I drew from eleven interviews conducted between 2003 and 2008 with women who had been active in NOW or one of its schisms.

Finally, I located a publicly available interview with Judith Lonnquist conducted by the Washington Women's History Consortium in 2007, in which she was asked about factionalism in NOW and her strategies for coping with it.

There is some overlap in these sets of interviews, which is why there are more interviews than interviewees. I interviewed Mary Eastwood and Elizabeth Farians, two activists who also participated in the Tully–Crenshaw Project. Gloria Steinem participated in both the Tully–Crenshaw and Voices of Feminism projects. In each case, I drew from both interview transcripts.

Across all sources, interviewees are mostly white women from middle-class backgrounds and ranged in age from their mid-thirties to their late eighties at the time of the interviews. Most of them were active in the early years of NOW, and they varied in how long they stayed active in the organization, from just three years to several decades. Others were active only in the schism organization that split from NOW. Given the span of time between the actual events and when the interviews were conducted, we should consider issues of reliability and validity in these data. Where possible, I triangulated data between the interviews, archival sources, and histories of the movement to confirm accounts. Where there are discrepancies between accounts, I present all perspectives of what occurred. The NOW archive (described later) proved an invaluable source of contemporaneous reports and correspondence exchanged by activists and offers a check on the accounts offered in activist interviews.

Interview Subjects (Source in Parentheses)

1. Dolores Alexander (Voices of Feminism)
2. Judith Berek (Voices of Feminism)
3. Betty Berry (Tully–Crenshaw)
4. Joan E. Biren (Voices of Feminism)
5. Rosemary Oelrich Bottcher (author interview)
6. Gene Boyer (Tully–Crenshaw)
7. Toni Carabillo (Tully–Crenshaw)
8. Jacqueline Ceballos (author interview)
9. Candi Churchill (author interview)
10. Mary Jean Collins (author interview)
11. Judith Lightfoot Cormack (Tully–Crenshaw)
12. Carol Crossed (author interview)
13. Karen DeCrow (Tully–Crenshaw)
14. Merrillee Dolan (Tully–Crenshaw)
15. Mary Eastwood (Tully–Crenshaw; author interview)
16. Joanne Edgar (Voices of Feminism)
17. Elizabeth Farians (Tully–Crenshaw; author interview)
18. Jean Faust (Tully–Crenshaw)
19. Shelley Fernandez (author interview)
20. Muriel Fox (author interview)
21. Arvonne Fraser (author interview)
22. Betty Friedan (Tully–Crenshaw)
23. Cynthia Fuchs-Epstein (Tully–Crenshaw)
24. Patricia Goltz (author interview)
25. Wilma Scott Heide (Tully–Crenshaw)

26. Florynce Kennedy (Tully–Crenshaw)
27. Frances Kissling (author interview)
28. Judith Lonnquist (Washington Women's History Consortium)
29. Barbara Love (Voices of Feminism)
30. Rachel MacNair (author interview)
31. Erin Matson (author interview)
32. Judith Meuli (Tully–Crenshaw)
33. Geraldine Miller (Voices of Feminism)
34. Achebe Betty Powell (Voices of Feminism)
35. Minnie Bruce Pratt (Voices of Feminism)
36. Loretta Ross (Voices of Feminism)
37. Alice Rossi (Tully–Crenshaw)
38. Bernice Sandler (author interview)
39. Martha Shelley (Voices of Feminism)
40. Gloria Steinem (Tully–Crenshaw; Voices of Feminism)
41. Mary Jean Tully (Tully–Crenshaw)
42. Molly Yard (Tully–Crenshaw)

Interview Schedules

The following schedules provide the general template of questions I asked in the interviews. Each interview varied and included additional questions tailored to the interviewee's specific organization and her answers to these questions.

Semistructured Interview Guide—Organizational Split Version

1. Can you tell me how you became involved in [NOW/new group/both]?
2. Have you held any official positions in [group]?
3. How important has [group] been to your everyday life?
4. How much time do you devote to [group] per day? Per week?
5. Are/were you involved in organizations other than [group]?
6. Did you hold any positions in the other organization(s)?
7. Can you tell me the story about [episode of factionalism]?
8. What would you say were the main reasons for wanting to form a new organization? (probes: goals, priorities, tactics, targets, structural differences)
9. What were the specific events that led up to the episode of factionalism?
10. How many people would you say were involved in your group (faction)?
11. How did (other) NOW leaders respond to these things?
12. At what point did you start thinking about forming a new organization?

13. Did other leaders or members try to prevent you from leaving or starting a new organization?

14. Was there an overlap in membership between NOW and [new organization]?

15. Did NOW ever offer any resources to your new organization? (probe: financial, material, symbolic)

16. Were there other organizations or individuals outside of NOW who assisted you as you were forming the new organization? (probes: office space, financial, material, advice)

17. If so, how did those organizations get involved?

18. Did you stay a member of NOW?

19. From what you know, did NOW change after the new organization was formed? Did it form special committees or change policies related to these issues?

20. How much communication was there between NOW and [new group] after the split/founding? (probes: common projects, advice, collaboration, membership overlap)

21. How long did you stay involved with [new group]? Why did you leave the organization?

Semistructured Interview Guide—Factionalism/Nonsplit Version

1. Can you tell me about how you became involved in NOW?

2. Were you involved in organizations other than NOW?

3. Did you hold any positions in the other organization(s)?

4. How important has NOW been to your everyday life?

5. How much time do you devote to NOW per day? Per week?

6. Has your level of involvement changed over time? (probes: more or less involved now)

7. Have you held any official positions in NOW?

8. Can you tell me the story about [episode of factionalism]?

9. Were there specific events that happened that led up to the conflict?

10. What would you say were the main reasons for wanting to form a new organization? (probes: goals, priorities, tactics, targets, structural differences)

11. How many people would you say were involved in your group?

12. How did (other) NOW leaders respond to these things?

13. Was the response from NOW leadership satisfying? Why or why not?

14. Did people in your group disagree over how to respond?

15. Did your group ever consider leaving NOW over this issue?

16. Did some members leave NOW over the issue? If so, who were they? (probes: how many, paid staff, informal leaders)

17. Where did they go? (probes: joined a different group, started their own group, dropped out completely)
18. Were any efforts made to prevent you from leaving or starting a new organization? (probes: by NOW leaders, by other members)
19. During the episode of factionalism, were other outside groups involved? (probes: people or organizations that encouraged or offered support)
20. If so, how did they get involved?
21. Of those members initially involved in the group, how many would you say continued to be involved in NOW for a significant amount of time afterward?

Archives

I collected archival data from the Schlesinger Library at Harvard University and the Sophia Smith Collection at Smith College. I selected documents based on the libraries' subject guides, which often indicated where there was material relevant to NOW's factions and organizational splits. These documents included correspondence sent from factions to NOW members, members' letters and reports to the board, and personal correspondence between leaders. I also drew from the research notes archived by Maren Lockwood Carden, a sociologist who collected information on factionalism in NOW. Her papers include "notes, memoranda, and printed material about dissent" in NOW, particularly about the Womansurge–Majority Caucus split on the national board of directors.

Collections List from Schlesinger Library, Radcliffe Institute, Harvard University, Cambridge, Massachusetts

1. National Organization for Women Records, 1959–2002 (including the following series: Organization and Policy; National Board Minutes; Political Action Committees, 1977–1996; Task Forces and Conference Implementation Committees, 1964–1991; NOW LDEF, 1973–1975; National Women's Political Caucus, 1975; Jean Faust's Files, 1967–1970, 1990; Papers of Leaders: Gene Boyer, 1961, 1966–1976; Papers of Leaders: Mary Anne Sedey, 1973–1976; Women's Equity Action League Records, 1967–1990)
2. Marguerite Rawalt Papers, 1870s–1989
3. *Electric Circle* 1, no. 1 (August 1975)
4. Human Rights for Women Records, 1966–1978
5. Catholics for a [Free] Choice
6. Toni Carabillo and Judith Meuli Papers, ca. 1890–2008

7. Mary O. Eastwood Papers, 1915–1983
8. Elizabeth Farians Papers, 1942–2013
9. Charlotte Bunch Papers, 1967–1985
10. Maren Lockwood Carden Papers, 1969–1979

Collections List from Sophia Smith Collection, Smith College, Northampton, Massachusetts

1. Loretta J. Ross Papers, 1956–2013

Newsletters, Manuals, and Collections Accessed Online

1. National Women's Liberation Newsletter, 2011–2012, http://www
   .womensliberation.org/index.php/about/newsletters
2. National Organization for Women Administrative Policy Manual, 1966–
   1996, https://now.org/wp-content/uploads/2014/01/NOW-Administrative
   -Policy-Manual-1966-1996.pdf
3. National Organization for Women Administrative Policy Manual,
   1997–October 2014, https://now.org/wp-content/uploads/2015/05/NOW
   -Admin-Policy-Manual-Addendum-1997-October-2014.pdf
4. National Organization for Women Issues Policy Manual, A through L,
   1966–1996, https://now.org/wp-content/uploads/2014/01/NOW-Issues
   -A-L-Policy-Manual-1966-1996.pdf
5. National Organization for Women Issues Policy Manual, M through Z,
   1966–1996, https://now.org/wp-content/uploads/2014/01/NOW-Issues
   -M-Z-Policy-Manual-1966-1996.pdf
6. National Organization for Women Issues Policy Manual Addendum,
   1997–October 2014, https://now.org/wp-content/uploads/2015/05/NOW
   -Issues-Policy-Manual-Addendum-1997-October-2014.pdf
7. *Conscience,* Catholics for [a Free] Choice quarterly journal, from winter
   1996/1997 through summer 2004
8. *The American Feminist,* Feminists for Life journal, from winter 1997/1998
   through winter 2004/2005
9. *SisterLife* 1 and 2, Feminists for Life newsletter (precursor to *The
   American Feminist*)

Secondary Sources

Existing biographies, memoirs, histories, and academic accounts of the feminist movement informed this study. In some cases, they detailed cases of factionalism and splitting I would not have found otherwise. Following is a list, though not exhaustive, of works that were particularly helpful in uncovering new cases of these phenomena and filling in the details.

Atkinson, Ti-Grace. *Amazon Odyssey: The First Collection of Writings by the Political Pioneer of the Women's Movement.* New York: Links Books, 1974.

Banaszak, Lee Ann. *The Women's Movement Inside and Outside the State.* New York: Cambridge University Press, 2010.

Barakso, Maryann. *Governing NOW: Grassroots Activism in the National Organization for Women.* Ithaca, N.Y.: Cornell University Press, 2004.

Brown, Rita Mae. *A Plain Brown Rapper.* Oakland, Calif.: Diana Press, 1976.

Brown, Rita Mae. *Rita Will: Memoir of a Literary Rabble-Rouser.* New York: Bantam Books, 1997.

Carden, Maren L. *The New Feminist Movement.* New York: Sage Press, 1974.

Cohen, Marcia. *The Sisterhood: The True Story of the Women Who Changed the World.* New York: Simon and Schuster, 1988.

Davis, Flora. *Moving the Mountain: The Women's Movement in America since 1960.* Chicago: University of Illinois Press, 1999.

Derr, Mary Krane, Rachel MacNair, and Linda Naranjo-Huebl. *Prolife Feminism: Yesterday and Today.* Kansas City, Mo.: Feminism and Nonviolence Studies Association, 2005.

Echols, Alice. *Daring to Be Bad: Radical Feminism in America, 1967–1975.* Minneapolis: University of Minnesota Press, 1989.

Fraser, Arvonne. *She's No Lady: Politics, Family, and International Feminism.* Minneapolis, Minn.: Nodin Press, 2007.

Freeman, Jo. *The Politics of Women's Liberation: A Case Study of an Emerging Social Movement and Its Relation to the Policy Process.* New York: Longman, 2000.

Friedan, Betty. *It Changed My Life: Writings on the Women's Movement.* New York: Random House, 1976.

Gilmore, Stephanie. *Groundswell: Grassroots Feminist Activism in Postwar America.* New York: Routledge, 2013.

Henold, Mary J. *Catholic and Feminist: The Surprising History of the American Catholic Feminist Movement.* Chapel Hill: University of North Carolina Press, 2008.

Huckle, Patricia. *Tish Sommers, Activist, and the Founding of the Older Women's League.* Knoxville: University of Tennessee Press, 1991.

Marotta, Toby. *The Politics of Homosexuality.* Boston: Houghton Mifflin, 1981.

Oshima, Toko. *"Sisterhood Is Powerful. It Kills Sisters": Ti-Grace Atkinson and the Feminists.* Bronxville, N.Y.: Women's History, Sarah Lawrence College, 1995.

Sherman, Janann. *Interviews with Betty Friedan.* Jackson: University of Mississippi Press, 2002.

Slavin, Sarah, ed. *U.S. Women's Interest Groups: Institutional Profiles*. Westport, Conn.: Greenwood Press, 1995.

Springer, Kimberly. *Living for the Revolution: Black Feminist Organizations, 1968–1980*. Durham, N.C.: Duke University Press, 2005.

Zurakowski, Michele. *The Ephemeral Rhetoric of Ti-Grace Atkinson: Style and Strategy in Amazon Odyssey*. Minneapolis: University of Minnesota Press, 1989.

Akchurin, Maria, and Cheol-Sung Lee. 2013. "Pathways to Empowerment: Repertoires of Women's Activism and Gender Earnings Equality." *American Sociological Review* 78, no. 4: 679–701. https://doi.org/10.1177/0003122413494759.

Alcoff, Linda. 1988. "Cultural Feminism versus Post-structuralism: The Identity Crisis in Feminist Theory." *Signs: Journal of Women in Culture and Society* 13, no. 3: 405–36. https://doi.org/10.1086/494426.

Andrews, Kenneth T., Marshall Ganz, Matthew Baggetta, Hahrie Han, and Chaeyoon Lim. 2010. "Leadership, Membership, and Voice: Civic Associations That Work." *American Journal of Sociology* 115, no. 4: 1191–1242. https://doi.org/10.1086/649060.

Atkinson, Ti-Grace. 1974. *Amazon Odyssey: The First Collection of Writings by the Political Pioneer of the Women's Movement.* New York: Links Books.

Balser, Deborah B. 1997. "The Impact of Environmental Factors on Factionalism and Schism in Social Movement Organizations." *Social Forces* 76, no. 1: 199–228. https://doi.org/10.2307/2580323.

Banaszak, Lee Ann. 2010. *The Women's Movement Inside and Outside the State.* New York: Cambridge University Press.

Barakso, Maryann. 2004. *Governing NOW: Grassroots Activism in the National Organization for Women.* Ithaca, N.Y.: Cornell University Press.

Barkan, Steven E. 1986. "Interorganizational Conflict in the Southern Civil Rights Movement." *Sociological Inquiry* 56, no. 2: 190–209. https://doi.org/10.1111/j.1475-682X.1986.tb00083.x.

Bayless, Liza. 2016. "Americans Gave 'Unprecedented' Millions to Causes in Trump's Line of Fire." *YES! Magazine.* November 16. http://www.yesmagazine.org/people-power/americans-gave-unprecedented-millions-to-causes-in-trumps-line-of-fire-20161116.

BBC News. 2004. "Abortion Activists on the March." April 26. http://news.bbc
.co.uk/2/hi/americas/3657527.stm.

Benford, Robert D. 1993. "Frame Disputes within the Nuclear Disarmament Movement." *Social Forces* 71, no. 3: 677–701. https://doi.org/10.2307/2579890.

Berkhout, Joost. 2013. "Why Interest Organizations Do What They Do: Assessing the Explanatory Potential of 'Exchange' Approaches." *Interest Groups and
Advocacy* 2, no. 2: 227–50. https://doi.org/10.1057/iga.2013.6.

Blee, Kathleen M. 2012. *Democracy in the Making: How Activist Groups Form.*
New York: Oxford University Press.

Bonde, Helena, and Soph Bonde. 2017. "A Critical Look at the Women's March: A
Disability Perspective." *Argot Magazine.* January 27. http://www.argotmagazine
.com/first-person-and-perspectives/a-critical-look-at-the-womens-march-a
-disability-perspective.

Boris, Elizabeth T. 2006. "Introduction: Nonprofit Organizations in a Democracy:
Roles and Responsibilities." In *Nonprofits and Government: Collaboration and
Conflict,* edited by Elizabeth T. Boris and C. Eugene Steuerle, 1–36. Washington,
D.C.: Urban Insitute.

Boyer, Gene. 1991. Interview by Muriel Fox. Tully–Crenshaw Feminist Oral History Project Records, 1961–2001. MC 548, folder 1.8–1.10. Schlesinger Library, Radcliffe Institute, Harvard University, Cambridge, Mass.

Caniglia, Beth, and JoAnn Carmin. 2005. "Scholarship on Social Movement
Organizations: Classic Views and Emerging Trends." *Mobilization: An International Quarterly* 10, no. 2: 201–12. https://doi.org/10.17813/maiq.10.2
.q848h37832857t5j.

Carden, Maren Lockwood. 1974. *The New Feminist Movement.* New York: Russell
Sage Foundation.

Carmin, Joann, and Deborah B. Balser. 2002. "Selecting Repertoires of Action
in Environmental Movement Organizations: An Interpretive Approach."
Organization and Environment 15, no. 4: 365–88. https://doi.org/10.1177
/1086026602238167.

Carroll, Glenn R. 1984. "Organizational Ecology." *Annual Review of Sociology*
10, no. 1: 71–93. https://doi.org/10.1146/annurev.so.10.080184.000443.

Carroll, Glenn R. 1985. "Concentration and Specialization: Dynamics of Niche
Width in Populations of Organizations." *American Journal of Sociology* 90,
no. 6: 1262–83.

Carroll, Glenn R., and Anand Swaminathan. 2000. "Why the Microbrewery Movement? Organizational Dynamics of Resource Partitioning in the U.S. Brewing Industry." *American Journal of Sociology* 106, no. 3: 715–62. https://doi.org/10
.1086/318962.

Cauterucci, Christina. 2016. "Thousands Are Planning to Go to the Women's March
on Washington. But Will It Actually Happen?" *Slate Magazine.* November 23.

http://www.slate.com/articles/life/doublex/2016/11/the_women_s_march_on
_washington_faces_uncertain_logistics_on_inauguration.html.

Chapin, F. Stuart, and John E. Tsouderos. 1956. "The Formalization Process in
Voluntary Associations." *Social Forces* 34, no. 4: 342–44. https://doi.org/10
.2307/2573667.

Chen, Katherine K., Howard Lune, and Edward L. Queen. 2013. "How Values
Shape and Are Shaped by Nonprofit and Voluntary Organizations: The Current State of the Field." *Nonprofit and Voluntary Sector Quarterly* 42, no. 5:
856–85. https://doi.org/10.1177/0899764013480273.

Chira, Susan. 2018. "The Women's March Became a Movement. What's Next?" *New
York Times.* January 20. https://www.nytimes.com/2018/01/20/us/womens
-march-metoo.html.

Choi-Fitzpatrick, Austin. 2015. "Managing Democracy in Social Movement Organizations." *Social Movement Studies* 14, no. 2: 123–41. https://doi.org/10
.1080/14742837.2014.945158.

Clemens, Elisabeth S. 1993. "Organizational Repertoires and Institutional Change:
Women's Groups and the Transformation of U.S. Politics, 1890–1920." *American Journal of Sociology* 98, no. 4: 755–98.

Cobb, Jelani. 2016. "Where Is Black Lives Matter Headed?" *The New Yorker.*
March 7. https://www.newyorker.com/magazine/2016/03/14/where-is-black
-lives-matter-headed.

Cohen, Marcia. 1988. *The Sisterhood: The True Story of the Women Who
Changed the World.* New York: Simon and Schuster.

Cooper, Arnold C., and F. Javier Gimeno Gascon. 1992. "Entrepreneurs, Processes
of Founding, and New Firm Performance." In *The State of the Art of Entrepreneurship,* edited by Donald L. Sexton and John D. Kasarda, 301–40. Boston:
PWS Kent.

Coser, Lewis A. 1956. *The Functions of Social Conflict.* New York: Routledge.

Costain, Anne N., and W. Douglas Costain. 1987. "Strategies and Tactics of the
Women's Movement of the United States: The Role of Political Parties." In *The
Women's Movements of the United States and Western Europe: Consciousness,
Political Opportunity, and Public Policy,* edited by Mary Fainsod Katzenstein
and Carol Mueller, 196–214. Philadelphia: Temple University Press.

Crockett, Emily. 2016. "The 'Women's March on Washington,' Explained." *Vox.*
November 21. https://www.vox.com/identities/2016/11/21/13651804/women
-march-washington-trump-inauguration.

Cuddy, Bob. 2011. "Rowdy Behavior Leads to Schism in Occupy SLO Movement."
Tribune. October 26. http://www.sanluisobispo.com/news/local/article39187026
.html.

Cummings, Cecilia. 1982. "Minority Members of NOW Consider Forming Own
Group." *Indianapolis Star.* October 11.

Cusumano, Katherine. 2017. "The Women of the Women's March: Meet the Activists Who Are Planning One of the Largest Demonstrations in American History." *W Magazine.* January 19. https://www.wmagazine.com/story/womens-march-on-washington-activists-organizers.

Davis, Flora. 1999. *Moving the Mountain: The Women's Movement in America since 1960.* Chicago: University of Illinois Press.

Davis, Gerald F., Doug McAdam, W. Richard Scott, and Mayer N. Zald. 2005. *Social Movements and Organization Theory.* New York: Cambridge University Press.

DeCrow, Karen. 1981. Interview by Frances Kolb. Tully–Crenshaw Feminist Oral History Project Records, MC 548, folder 2.10. Schlesinger Library, Radcliffe Institute, Harvard University, Cambridge, Mass.

Disney, Jennifer Leigh, and Joyce Gelb. 2000. "Feminist Organizational 'Success': The State of US Women's Movement Organizations in the 1990s." *Women and Politics* 21, no. 3: 39–76.

Dowding, Keith, Peter John, Thanos Mergoupis, and Mark Vugt. 2000. "Exit, Voice and Loyalty: Analytic and Empirical Developments." *European Journal of Political Research* 37, no. 4: 469–95. https://doi.org/10.1111/1475-6765.00522.

Downey, Gary L. 1986. "Ideology and the Clamshell Identity: Organizational Dilemmas in the Anti–Nuclear Power Movement." *Social Problems* 33, no. 5: 357–73. https://doi.org/10.2307/800656.

Dubois. 2011. "Occupy Wall Street: Yes, There Is Organization." Fortune. December 7. http://fortune.com/2011/12/07/occupy-wall-street-yes-there-is-organization/.

Dyck, B. 1997. "Exploring Organizational Family Trees: A Multigenerational Approach for Studying Organizational Births." *Journal of Management Inquiry* 6, no. 3: 222–33. https://doi.org/10.1177/105649269763007.

Dyck, Bruno, and Frederick A. Starke. 1999. "The Formation of Breakaway Organizations: Observations and a Process Model." *Administrative Science Quarterly* 44, no. 4: 792–822. https://doi.org/10.2307/2667056.

Earthjustice. 1997. "Sierra Club Legal Defense Fund Changes Name to Earthjustice Legal Defense Fund." June 14. http://earthjustice.org/news/press/1997/sierra-club-legal-defense-fund-changes-name-to-earthjustice-legal-defense-fund.

Eastwood, Mary. 1992. Interview by Muriel Fox. Tully–Crenshaw Feminist Oral History Project Records, 1961–2001. MC 548, folder 3.4–3.7. Schlesinger Library, Radcliffe Institute, Harvard University, Cambridge, Mass.

Echols, Alice. 1983. "Cultural Feminism: Feminist Capitalism and the Anti-pornography Movement." *Social Text,* no. 7: 34–53. https://doi.org/10.2307/466453.

Echols, Alice. 1989. *Daring to Be Bad: Radical Feminism in America, 1967–1975.* Minneapolis: University of Minnesota Press.

Edwards, Bob, and Sam Marullo. 1995. "Organizational Mortality in a Declining

Social Movement: The Demise of Peace Movement Organizations in the End of the Cold War Era." *American Sociological Review* 60, no. 6: 908–27. https://doi.org/10.2307/2096432.

Electric Circle. 1975. "Toward a Feminist Ethos."

Elizabeth Farians Papers. 1972. "Joint Committee of Organizations Brochure." MC 480, folder 2.7. Schlesinger Library, Radcliffe Institute, Harvard University, Cambridge, Mass.

Faludi, Susan. 2013. "Death of a Revolutionary." *The New Yorker.* April 15. http://www.newyorker.com/magazine/2013/04/15/death-of-a-revolutionary.

Farians, Elizabeth. 1997. Interview by Jacqueline Michot Ceballos. Tully–Crenshaw Feminist Oral History Project Records, MC 548, folder 4.1. Schlesinger Library, Radcliffe Institute, Harvard University, Cambridge, Mass.

Faust, Jean. 1990. Interview by Julie Altman. Tully–Crenshaw Feminist Oral History Project Records, MC 548, folder 4.5. Schlesinger Library, Radcliffe Institute, Harvard University, Cambridge, Mass.

Felsenthal, Julia. 2017. "These Are the Women Organizing the Women's March on Washington." *Vogue.* January 10. http://www.vogue.com/article/meet-the-women-of-the-womens-march-on-washington.

Ferree, Myra Marx, and Beth Hess. 2000. *Controversy and Coalition: The New Feminist Movement across Four Decades of Change.* New York: Routledge.

Ferree, Myra Marx, and Patricia Yancey Martin. 1995. *Feminist Organizations: Harvest of the New Women's Movement.* Philadelphia: Temple University Press.

Fetner, Tina. 2008. *How the Religious Right Shaped Lesbian and Gay Activism.* Minneapolis: University of Minnesota Press.

Fitzgerald, Kathleen J., and Diane M. Rodgers. 2000. "Radical Social Movement Organizations: A Theoretical Model." *Sociological Quarterly* 41, no. 4: 573–92. https://doi.org/10.1111/j.1533-8525.2000.tb00074.x.

Fligstein, Neil, and Doug McAdam. 2012. *A Theory of Fields.* New York: Oxford University Press.

Fortini, Amanda. 2018. "Fault Lines at the National Women's March, in Las Vegas." *The New Yorker.* January 23. https://www.newyorker.com/news/news-desk/fault-lines-at-the-national-womens-march-in-las-vegas.

Freeman, Jo. 1972. "The Tyranny of Structurelessness." *Berkeley Journal of Sociology* 17: 151–64.

Freeman, Jo. 1975. "Political Organization in the Feminist Movement." *Acta Sociologica* 18, no. 2–3: 222–44.

Freeman, Jo. 2000. *The Politics of Women's Liberation: A Case Study of an Emerging Social Movement and Its Relation to the Policy Process.* New York: Longman.

Frey, R. Scott, Thomas Dietz, and Linda Kalof. 1992. "Characteristics of Successful American Protest Groups: Another Look at Gamson's Strategy of Social

Protest." *American Journal of Sociology* 98, no. 2: 368–87. https://doi.org/10 .1086/230012.

Friedan, Betty. 1998. *It Changed My Life: Writings on the Women's Movement.* Cambridge, Mass.: Harvard University Press.

Friedan, Betty. 2000. *Life So Far: A Memoir.* New York, N.Y.: Simon and Schuster.

Friedersdorf, Conor. 2017. "The Significance of Millions in the Streets." *The Atlantic.* January 23. https://www.theatlantic.com/politics/archive/2017/01/the -significance-of-millions-in-the-streets/514091/.

Gainesville NOW Newsletter. 2000. "Spark! Voices and Views of NOW Feminists." No. 4.

Gamson, Joshua. 1997. "Messages of Exclusion: Gender, Movements, and Symbolic Boundaries." *Gender and Society* 11, no. 2: 178–99. https://doi.org/10.1177 /089124397011002003.

Gamson, William A. 1990. *The Strategy of Social Protest.* Belmont, N.Y.: Wadsworth.

Garcia, Sandra E. 2017. "The Woman Who Created #MeToo Long Before Hashtags." *New York Times.* October 20. https://www.nytimes.com/2017/10 /20/us/me-too-movement-tarana-burke.html.

Gautney, Heather. 2011. "What Is Occupy Wall Street? The History of Leaderless Movements." *Washington Post.* October 10. https://www.washingtonpost .com/national/on-leadership/what-is-occupy-wall-street-the-history-of -leaderless-movements/2011/10/10/gIQAwkFjaL_story.html.

Gerlach, Luther P., and Virginia H. Hine. 1970. *People, Power, Change: Movements of Social Transformation.* Indianapolis, Ind.: Bobbs-Merrill.

Ghaziani, Amin. 2008. *The Dividends of Dissent: How Conflict and Culture Work in Lesbian and Gay Marches on Washington.* Chicago: University of Chicago Press.

Gillham, Patrick F., and Bob Edwards. 2011. "Legitimacy Management, Preservation of Exchange Relationships, and the Dissolution of the Mobilization for Global Justice Coalition." *Social Problems* 58, no. 3: 433–60. https://doi.org /10.1525/sp.2011.58.3.433.

Gilmore, Stephanie. 2013. *Groundswell: Grassroots Feminist Activism in Postwar America.* New York: Routledge.

Gilmore, Stephanie, and Elizabeth Kaminski. 2007. "A Part and Apart: Lesbian and Straight Feminist Activists Negotiate Identity in a Second-Wave Organization." *Journal of the History of Sexuality* 16, no. 1: 95–113.

Glaser, Barney. 2017. *Discovery of Grounded Theory: Strategies for Qualitative Research.* New York: Routledge.

Greer, Evan. 2017. "The Women's March Left Trans Women Behind." *Advocate.* January 25. http://www.advocate.com/commentary/2017/1/25/womens-march -left-trans-women-behind.

Guevarra, Ericka Cruz. n.d. "Portland Women's March Takes New Approach in 2018." https://www.opb.org/news/article/portland-womens-march-canceled -2018/.

Haines, Herbert H. 1984. "Black Radicalization and the Funding of Civil Rights: 1957–1970." *Social Problems* 32, no. 1: 31–43. https://doi.org/10.2307 /800260.

Halper, Evan. 2017. "A New Generation of Democrats Isn't Waiting for the Party to Tell It What to Do." *Los Angeles Times.* June 9. http://www.latimes.com /politics/la-na-pol-democrats-recruiting-20170609-story.html.

Hanna, Mary T. 1979. *Catholics and American Politics.* Cambridge, Mass.: Harvard University Press.

Hannan, Michael T., and John Freeman. 1988. "The Ecology of Organizational Mortality: American Labor Unions, 1836–1985." *American Journal of Sociology* 94, no. 1: 25–52. https://doi.org/10.1086/228950.

Hillman, Amy J., Michael C. Withers, and Brian J. Collins. 2009. "Resource Dependence Theory: A Review." *Journal of Management* 35, no. 6: 1404–27. https://doi.org/10.1177/0149206309343469.

Hirschman, Albert O. 1970. *Exit, Voice, and Loyalty: Responses to Decline in Firms, Organizations, and States.* Cambridge, Mass.: Harvard University Press.

Huckle, Patricia. 1991. *Tish Sommers, Activist, and the Founding of the Older Women's League.* Knoxville: University of Tennessee Press.

Hunt, Scott A., Robert D. Benford, and David A. Snow. 1994. "Identity Fields: Framing Processes and the Social Construction of Movement Identities." In *New Social Movements: From Ideology to Identity,* edited by Enrique Larana, Hank Johnston, and Joseph R. Gusfield, 185–208. Philadelphia: Temple University Press.

Janofsky, Michael. 1997. "At Million Woman March, Focus Is on Family." *New York Times.* October 26. https://www.nytimes.com/1997/10/26/us/at-million -woman-march-focus-is-on-family.html.

Jasper, James. 2004. "A Strategic Approach to Collective Action: Looking for Agency in Social-Movement Choices." *Mobilization: An International Quarterly* 9, no. 1: 1–16. https://doi.org/10.17813/maiq.9.1.m112677546p63361.

Jasper, James M. 2008. *The Art of Moral Protest: Culture, Biography, and Creativity in Social Movements.* Chicago: University of Chicago Press.

Jenkins, J. Craig. 1983. "Resource Mobilization Theory and the Study of Social Movements." *Annual Review of Sociology* 9, no. 1: 527–53. https://doi.org/10 .1146/annurev.so.09.080183.002523.

Joseph, Peniel. 2017. "One Scholar on the Future of Black Lives Matter." Interview by Robin Young. http://www.wbur.org/hereandnow/2017/04/05/peniel -joseph-black-lives-matter.

Kahn, Mattie. 2017. "The Women's March on Washington: How It Came to

Be and What You Need to Know." *ELLE.* January 12. http://www.elle.com /culture/news/a42067/womens-march-on-washington-timeline-logistics/.

Kaufman, Marc. 2005. "9 Arrested Protesting Morning-After Pill Plan." *Washington Post.* January 8, sec. A03.

King, Leslie. 2008. "Ideology, Strategy, and Conflict in a Social Movement Organization: The Sierra Club Immigration Wars." *Mobilization: An International Quarterly* 13, no. 1: 45–61. https://doi.org/10.17813/maiq.13.1.c7pv26280665g90g.

Kretschmer, Kelsy. 2009. "Contested Loyalties: Dissident Identity Organizations, Institutions, and Social Movements." *Sociological Perspectives* 52, no. 4: 433–54. https://doi.org/10.1525/sop.2009.52.4.433.

Kretschmer, Kelsy. 2014. "Shifting Boundaries and Splintering Movements: Abortion Rights in the Feminist and New Right Movements." *Sociological Forum* 29, no. 4: 893–915. https://doi.org/10.1111/socf.12125.

Kretschmer, Kelsy, and Kristen Barber. 2016. "Men at the March: Feminist Movement Boundaries and Men's Participation in Take Back the Night and Slutwalk." *Mobilization: An International Quarterly* 21, no. 3: 283–300. https:// doi.org/10.17813/1086-671X-20-3-283.

Kretschmer, Kelsy, and Jane Mansbridge. 2017. "The Equal Rights Amendment Campaign and Its Opponents." In *The Oxford Handbook of U.S. Women's Social Movement Activism,* edited by Holly J. McCammon, Verta Taylor, Jo Reger, and Rachel L. Einwohner, 71–88. New York: Oxford University Press.

Kumar, Divya. 2017a. "New NOW President Found Activist Roots in Pinellas." *Tampa Bay Times.* October 11. http://www.tbo.com/news/humaninterest/new -now-president-found-activist-roots-in-pinellas/2340491.

Ladau, Emily. 2017. "Why Are Disability Rights Absent from the Women's March Platform?" *The Establishment.* January 16. https://theestablishment.co /disability-rights-are-conspicuously-absent-from-the-womens-march -platform-1d61cee62593.

LeBlanc-Ernest, Anglea Darlean. 2013. "Black Women Organized for Action." In *Organizing Black America,* edited by Nina Mjagkij, 113. New York: Routledge.

Levitsky, Sandra. 2007. "Niche Activism: Constructing a Unified Movement Identity in a Heterogeneous Organizational Field." *Mobilization: An International Quarterly* 12, no. 3: 271–86. https://doi.org/10.17813/maiq.12.3.3v020m3751v1k642.

Liebman, Robert C., John R. Sutton, and Robert Wuthnow. 1988. "Exploring the Social Sources of Denominationalism: Schisms in American Protestant Denominations, 1890–1980." *American Sociological Review* 53, no. 3: 343–52. https://doi.org/10.2307/2095643.

Lofland, John. 1996. *Social Movement Organizations: Guide to Research on Insurgent Realities.* New Brunswick, N.J.: Transaction.

Lonnquist, Judith. 2007. Interview by Mildred Andrews. International Women's Year Oral History Project. Washington Historical Society. http://www .washingtonhistory.org/research/whc/oralhistory/IWYOralHistory/.

Loretta J. Ross Papers. 1973. "To: Chapter Presidents, Task Force Coordinators (Minority Women/Women's Rights and National Board Members); From Patsy G. Fulcher, Aileen C. Hernandez, Eleanor Spikes Co-ordinators, Task Force on Minority Women/Women's Rights. September." MS 504, folder 24.5. Sophia Smith Collection, Smith College, Northampton, Mass.

Loretta J. Ross Papers. 1979. "Letter from Aileen C. Hernandez; Dear Friends." MS 504, folder 24.5. Sophia Smith Collection, Smith College, Northampton, Mass.

Loretta J. Ross Papers. 1980. "Dear Muriel, December." MS 504, folder 24.5. Sophia Smith Collection, Smith College, Northampton, Mass.

Love, Barbara J. 2006. *Feminists Who Changed America, 1963–1975*. Urbana: University of Illinois Press.

Luker, Kristin. 1985. *Abortion and the Politics of Motherhood*. Berkeley: University of California Press.

Luna, Zakiya T. 2010. "Marching toward Reproductive Justice: Coalitional (Re) Framing of the March for Women's Lives." *Sociological Inquiry* 80, no. 4: 554–78. https://doi.org/10.1111/j.1475-682X.2010.00349.x.

Maren Lockwood Carden Papers. 1975. "Dear NOW Chapter Presidents and State Coordinators." MC 504, folder 8.6. Schlesinger Library, Radcliffe Institute, Harvard University, Cambridge, Mass.

Marguerite Rawalt Papers. 1968. "Dear Marguerite, November 15." MC 478, folder 10.30. Schlesinger Library, Radcliffe Institute, Harvard University, Cambridge, Mass.

Marotta, Toby. 1981. *The Politics of Homosexuality*. Boston: Houghton Mifflin.

Martin, Patricia Yancey. 1990. "Rethinking Feminist Organizations." *Gender and Society* 4, no. 2: 182–206. https://doi.org/10.1177/089124390004002004.

Mary O. Eastwood Papers. 1968. "History of the Equality Issue in the Contemporary Women's Movement by Janine Sade." MC 596, folder 6.55. Schlesinger Library, Radcliffe Institute, Harvard University, Cambridge, Mass.

Mary O. Eastwood Papers. 1970a. "Letter to HRW Directors from Mary Eastwood, May 21." MC 596, folder 4.34. Schlesinger Library, Radcliffe Institute, Harvard University, Cambridge, Mass.

Mary O. Eastwood Papers. 1970b. "Board of Directors Meeting Minutes, July 25." MC 596, folder 4.34. Schlesinger Library, Radcliffe Institute, Harvard University, Cambridge, Mass.

Mascaro, Lisa. 2017. "Trump's Election Has Mobilized a Resistance Like No Other, but Will Democrats' Answer to the Tea Party Divide the Ranks?" *Los Angeles Times*. April 23. http://www.latimes.com/politics/la-na-pol-tea-party-democrats-20170423-story.html.

McAdam, Doug. 1982. *Political Process and the Development of Black Insurgency, 1930–1970*. Chicago: University of Chicago Press.

McCammon, Holly J., Erin M. Bergner, and Sandra C. Arch. 2015. "'Are You One

of Those Women?' Within-Movement Conflict, Radical Flank Effects, and Social Movement Political Outcomes." *Mobilization: An International Quarterly*
20, no. 2: 157–78. https://doi.org/10.17813/1086-671X-20-2-157.

McCarthy, John D. 2005. "Persistence and Change among Nationally Federated Or-
ganizations." In *Social Movements and Organization Theory*, edited by Gerald F.
Davis, Doug McAdam, W. Richard Scott, and Mayer N. Zald, 193–225. New
York: Cambridge University Press.

McCarthy, John D., David W. Britt, and Mark Wolfson. 1991. "The Institutional
Channeling of Social Movements by the State in the United States." *Research
in Social Movements, Conflicts, and Change* 13, no. 2: 273–97.

McCarthy, John D., and Edward T. Walker. 2004. "Alternative Organizational
Repertoires of Poor People's Social Movement Organizations." *Nonprofit and
Voluntary Sector Quarterly* 33, no. 3: 97–119. http://journals.sagepub.com/doi
/abs/10.1177/0899764004266200.

McCarthy, John D., and Mayer N. Zald. 1977. "Resource Mobilization and Social Movements: A Partial Theory." *American Journal of Sociology* 82, no. 6:
1212–41.

McCloskey, Michael. 2005. *In the Thick of It: My Life in the Sierra Club*. Washington, D.C.: Island Press.

McKeegan, Michele. 1992. *Abortion Politics: Mutiny in the Ranks of the Right*.
New York: Free Press.

McVeigh, Karen. 2011. "Wall Street Protesters Divided over Occupy Movement's
Demands." *The Guardian*. October 18. http://www.theguardian.com/world/2011
/oct/19/occupy-wall-street-protesters-divided.

Merton, Robert K. 1940. "Bureaucratic Structure and Personality." *Social Forces*
18, no. 4: 560–68. https://doi.org/10.2307/2570634.

Meyer, David S. 2004. "Protest and Political Opportunities." *Annual Review of
Sociology* 30, no. 1: 125–45. https://doi.org/10.1146/annurev.soc.30.012703
.110545.

Minkoff, Debra C. 1995. *Organizing for Equality: The Evolution of Women's and
Racial-Ethnic Organizations in America, 1955–1985*. New Brunswick, N.J.:
Rutgers University Press.

Mitchell, Robert Cameron. 1981. "From Elite Quarrel to Mass Movement." *Society* 18, no. 5: 76–84. https://doi.org/10.1007/BF02701330.

Mooney, Chris, Joe Heim, and Brady Dennis. 2017. "Climate March Draws Mas-
sive Crowd to D.C. in Sweltering Heat." *Washington Post*. April 29. https://
www.washingtonpost.com/national/health-science/climate-march-expected
-to-draw-massive-crowd-to-dc-in-sweltering-heat/2017/04/28/1bdf5e66-2c3a
-11e7-b605-33413c691853_story.html.

Morris, Aldon D. 1986. *The Origins of the Civil Rights Movement*. New York:
Simon and Schuster.

Mueller, Carol. 1995. "The Organizational Basis of Conflict in Contemporary Feminism." In *Feminist Organizations: Harvest of the New Women's Movement,* edited by Patricia Yancey Martin and Myra Marx Ferree, 263–75. Philadelphia: Temple University Press.

National Organization for Women. 2017. "NOW Launches New National Action Program." March 16. http://now.org/media-center/press-release/now-launches-new-national-action-program/.

National Organization for Women. 2018. "Leading Feminist Organizations Convene to Discuss Solutions for Sexual Harassment." https://now.org/media-center/press-release/leading-feminist-organizations-convene-summit-to-discuss-solutions-for-sexual-harassment/.

National Organization for Women. n.d.-a. "Administrative Policy Manual, 1966–1996." http://now.org/wp-content/uploads/2014/01/NOW-Administrative-Policy-Manual-1966-1996.pdf.

National Organization for Women. n.d.-b. "Administrative Policy Manual, 1997–October 2014." http://now.org/wp-content/uploads/2015/05/NOW-Admin-Policy-Manual-Addendum-1997-October-2014.pdf.

National Organization for Women. n.d.-c. "Bylaws." http://now.org/about/structure-and-bylaws/bylaws/.

National Organization for Women. n.d.-d. "Issues Policy Manual, 1966–1996." http://now.org/wp-content/uploads/2014/01/NOW-Issues-A-L-Policy-Manual-1966-1996.pdf.

National Organization for Women. n.d.-e. "Issues Policy Manual, 1997–October 2014 (Addendum)." http://now.org/wp-content/uploads/2015/05/NOW-Issues-Policy-Manual-Addendum-1997-October-2014.pdf.

National Organization for Women. n.d.-f. "NOW's Intrepid Awards Gala on July 17." http://now.org/media-center/press-release/national-organization-for-womens-intrepid-awards-gala-on-july-17/#.

National Organization for Women Foundation. 2017. "About the NOW Foundation." http://now.org/now-foundation/about-now-foundation/.

National Organization for Women Records. 1967a. "Board of Directors Meeting Minutes." MC 496, folder 2.2. Schlesinger Library, Radcliffe Institute, Harvard University, Cambridge, Mass.

National Organization for Women Records. 1967b. "Jean Faust Files, Legislative Office—Notes on Abortion Rights." MC 496, folder 56.2. Schlesinger Library, Radcliffe Institute, Harvard University, Cambridge, Mass.

National Organization for Women Records. 1968a. "Board Meeting Minutes, September 14–15." MC 496, folder 2.3. Schlesinger Library, Radcliffe Institute, Harvard University, Cambridge, Mass.

National Organization for Women Records. 1968b. "Jean Faust Files, Legislative Office—Summaries of NOW-NY, with Comments by Jean Faust." MC

496, folder 56.3. Schlesinger Library, Radcliffe Institute, Harvard University, Cambridge, Mass.

National Organization for Women Records. 1969. "Board of Directors Meeting Minutes, June 28–29." MC 496, folder 2.4. Schlesinger Library, Radcliffe Institute, Harvard University, Cambridge, Mass.

National Organization for Women Records. 1970. "Board of Directors Meeting Minutes." MC 496, folder 2.7. Schlesinger Library, Radcliffe Institute, Harvard University, Cambridge, Mass.

National Organization for Women Records. 1973. "Task Force Status Report, July." MC 496, folder 42.1. Schlesinger Library, Radcliffe Institute, Harvard University, Cambridge, Mass.

National Organization for Women Records. 1974a. "Below Is a Total to Date . . . October 17." MC 496, folder 42.2. Schlesinger Library, Radcliffe Institute, Harvard University, Cambridge, Mass.

National Organization for Women Records. 1974b. "Board Report—Task Force Coordinator, Feb. 23–5." MC 496, folder 42.2. Schlesinger Library, Radcliffe Institute, Harvard University, Cambridge, Mass.

National Organization for Women Records. 1974c. "Dear Stacey, March 11." MC 496, folder 42.2. Schlesinger Library, Radcliffe Institute, Harvard University, Cambridge, Mass.

National Organization for Women Records. 1974d. "From the Task Forces Team Re Report to Board and Recommendations on New Task Force Guidelines, October 28." MC 496, folder 42.2. Schlesinger Library, Radcliffe Institute, Harvard University, Cambridge, Mass.

National Organization for Women Records. 1974e. "Proposed National Task Force Guidelines, October 28." MC 496, folder 42.2. Schlesinger Library, Radcliffe Institute, Harvard University, Cambridge, Mass.

National Organization for Women Records. 1974f. "Report of the National Task Force Coordinators Caucus Meeting . . . , May 24." MC 496, folder 42.2. Schlesinger Library, Radcliffe Institute, Harvard University, Cambridge, Mass.

National Organization for Women Records. 1975a. "Decentralizing NOW by Bev Jones." MC 496, folder 38.36. Schlesinger Library, Radcliffe Institute, Harvard University, Cambridge, Mass.

National Organization for Women Records. 1975b. "Dissidents in NOW Organize." *Washington Star.* November 16. MC 496, folder 38.36. Schlesinger Library, Radcliffe Institute, Harvard University, Cambridge, Mass.

National Organization for Women Records. 1975c. "Memo to: Task Force Coordinators; From: Karen DeCrow, November 9." MC 496, folder 42.3. Schlesinger Library, Radcliffe Institute, Harvard University, Cambridge, Mass.

National Organization for Women Records. 1975d. "National Task Forces and Committees July 25." MC 496, folder 42.3. Schlesinger Library, Radcliffe Institute, Harvard University, Cambridge, Mass.

National Organization for Women Records. 1975e. "Notes Taken at Meeting of NOW National Task Force Coordinators, February 15–16." MC 496, folder 42.3. Schlesinger Library, Radcliffe Institute, Harvard University, Cambridge, Mass.

National Organization for Women Records. 1975f. "To: National Task Force Coordinators, From Lynne Darcy, Task Force Team. July 1975." MC 496, folder 42.3. Schlesinger Library, Radcliffe Institute, Harvard University, Cambridge, Mass.

National Organization for Women Records. 1976a. "February 1, 1976 Dear NOW Members (from Mary Lynne Myeres and Elaine Latourell)." Papers of Leaders: Mary Anne Sedey, MC 496, folder 38.36. Schlesinger Library, Radcliffe Institute, Harvard University, Cambridge, Mass.

National Organization for Women Records. 1976b. "To: National Board; From: Karen DeCrow, January 8." MC 496, folder 42.4. Schlesinger Library, Radcliffe Institute, Harvard University, Cambridge, Mass.

National Organization for Women Records. 1977a. "Report of the National Organization for Women Human Rights Board Committee Meeting, December 2." MC 496, folder 42.4. Schlesinger Library, Radcliffe Institute, Harvard University, Cambridge, Mass.

National Organization for Women Records. 1977b. "To: Jeane Bendorf, Membership Committee; From: Harriet Perl, CR Coordinator, October 16." MC 496, folder 42.4. Schlesinger Library, Radcliffe Institute, Harvard University, Cambridge, Mass.

National Organization for Women Records. 1977c. "To: NOW National Board of Directors; From: NOW Executive Committee, July 30." MC 496, folder 42.4. Schlesinger Library, Radcliffe Institute, Harvard University, Cambridge, Mass.

National Organization for Women Records. 1978a. "Societal Equality Committee, December 2." MC 496, folder 42.4. Schlesinger Library, Radcliffe Institute, Harvard University, Cambridge, Mass.

National Organization for Women Records. 1978b. "To: State Coordinators and National Board Members and Committee Chairs; From: The Societal Equality Committee, April 3." MC 496, folder 42.4. Schlesinger Library, Radcliffe Institute, Harvard University, Cambridge, Mass.

National Organization for Women Records. 1979a. "Conference Resolutions Political Committee." MC 496, folder 99.1. Schlesinger Library, Radcliffe Institute, Harvard University, Cambridge, Mass.

National Organization for Women Records. 1979b. "Introduction to PAC Manual." MC 496, folder 99.1. Schlesinger Library, Radcliffe Institute, Harvard University, Cambridge, Mass.

National Organization for Women Records. 1979c. "NOW PAC Meeting Minutes Washington DC Apr 7–8." MC 496, folder 99.1. Schlesinger Library, Radcliffe Institute, Harvard University, Cambridge, Mass.

National Organization for Women Records. 1979d. "Report of the National Organization for Women Human Rights Board Committee Meeting, May 19." MC 496, folder 42.4. Schlesinger Library, Radcliffe Institute, Harvard University, Cambridge, Mass.

National Organization for Women Records. 1984. "PAC Manual—What Is a PAC?" MC 496, folder 99.3. Schlesinger Library, Radcliffe Institute, Harvard University, Cambridge, Mass.

National Organization for Women Records. n.d.-a. "Suggested Guidelines for Creation and Maintaining of Taskforces." MC 496, folder 42.7. Schlesinger Library, Radcliffe Institute, Harvard University, Cambridge, Mass.

National Organization for Women Records. n.d.-b. "Task Force on Task Forces—Report and Recommendations." MC 496, folder 42.4. Schlesinger Library, Radcliffe Institute, Harvard University, Cambridge, Mass.

National Organization for Women Records. n.d.-c. "To: Societal Equality Committee of the National Board from Mary Ellen Verheyden-Hilliard." MC 496, folder 42.4. Schlesinger Library, Radcliffe Institute, Harvard University, Cambridge, Mass.

Newman, Andy. 2017. "Highlights: Reaction to Trump's Travel Ban." *New York Times.* January 29. https://www.nytimes.com/2017/01/29/nyregion/trump-travel-ban-protests-briefing.html.

NOW Legal Defense and Education Fund Records. 1970. "Admin of the NOW Legal Defense Fund." MC 623, folder 1.16. Schlesinger Library, Radcliffe Institute, Harvard University, Cambridge, Mass.

NOW Legal Defense and Education Fund Records. 1979. "Comments at Meeting of Officers of NOW and NOW-LDEF at Fox Home August 29–30." MC 623, folder 1.14. Schlesinger Library, Radcliffe Institute, Harvard University, Cambridge, Mass.

NOW Legal Defense and Education Fund Records. n.d.-a. "A Guide to Using NOW LDEF." MC 623, folder 1.14. Schlesinger Library, Radcliffe Institute, Harvard University, Cambridge, Mass.

NOW Legal Defense and Education Fund Records. n.d.-b. "To the Board of NOW from Marilyn Hall Patel." MC 623, folder 1.14. Schlesinger Library, Radcliffe Institute, Harvard University, Cambridge, Mass.

Paterson, Judith Hillman. 1986. *Be Somebody: A Biography of Marguerite Rawalt.* Austin, Tex.: Eakin Press.

Perrow, Charles. 1986. *Complex Organizations: A Critical Essay.* New York: Random House.

Piven, Frances Fox, and Richard Cloward. 1977. *Poor People's Movements: Why They Succeed, How They Fail.* New York: Pantheon Books.

Polletta, Francesca. 2002. *Freedom Is an Endless Meeting: Democracy in American Social Movements.* Chicago: University of Chicago Press.

Polletta, Francesca. 2005. "How Participatory Democracy Became White: Culture and Organizational Choice." *Mobilization: An International Quarterly* 10, no. 2: 271–88. http://mobilizationjournal.org/doi/abs/10.17813/maiq.10.2.

Pomerleau, Clark A. 2010. "Empowering Members, Not Overpowering Them: The National Organization for Women, Calls for Lesbian Inclusion, and California Influence, 1960s–1980s." *Journal of Homosexuality* 57, no. 7: 842–61. https://doi.org/10.1080/00918369.2010.493414.

Postrel, Virginia. 1990. "The Green Road to Serfdom." http://reason.com/archives/1990/04/01/the-green-road-to-serfdom.

Pratt, Minnie Bruce. 2005. Interview by Kelly Anderson. Voices of Feminism Oral History Project, Sophia Smith Collection, Smith College, Northampton, Mass. https://www.smith.edu/libraries/libs/ssc/vof/transcripts/Pratt.pdf.

Reger, Jo. 2002a. "More Than One Feminism: Organizational Structure and the Construction of Collective Identity." In *Social Movements: Identity, Culture, and the State,* edited by David S. Meyer, Nancy Whittier, and Belinda Robnett, 171–84. New York: Oxford University Press.

Reger, Jo. 2002b. "Organizational Dynamics and Construction of Multiple Feminist Identities in the National Organization for Women." *Gender and Society* 16, no. 5: 710–27. https://doi.org/10.1177/089124302236993.

Reger, Jo. 2008. "Drawing Identity Boundaries: The Creation of Contemporary Feminism." In *Identity Work in Social Movements,* edited by Jo Reger, Daniel J. Myers, and Rachel L. Einwohner, 101–20. Minneapolis: University of Minnesota Press.

Reger, Jo. 2012. *Everywhere and Nowhere: Contemporary Feminism in the United States.* New York: Oxford University Press.

Reger, Jo, and Suzanne Staggenborg. 2006. "Patterns of Mobilization in Local Movement Organizations: Leadership and Strategy in Four National Organization for Women Chapters." *Sociological Perspectives* 49, no. 3: 297–323. https://doi.org/10.1525/sop.2006.49.3.297.

Reid, Elizabeth J. 2006. "Advocacy and the Challenges It Presents for Nonprofits." In *Nonprofits and Government: Collaboration and Conflict,* edited by Elizabeth T. Boris and C. Eugene Steuerle, 343–72. Washington, D.C.: Urban Insitute.

Ross, Loretta. 2004. Interview by Joyce Follett. Voices of Feminism Oral History Project. Sophia Smith Collection, Smith College, Northampton, MA. https://www.smith.edu/libraries/libs/ssc/vof/transcripts/Ross.pdf.

Rothschild-Whitt, Joyce. 1979. "The Collectivist Organization: An Alternative to Rational-Bureaucratic Models." *American Sociological Review* 44, no. 4: 509–27. https://doi.org/10.2307/2094585.

Ryan, Barbara. 1992. *Feminism and the Women's Movement: Dynamics of Change in Social Movement Ideology, and Activism.* New York: Routledge.

Sands, Darren. 2017. "What Happened to Black Lives Matter?" https://www
.buzzfeed.com/darrensands/what-happened-to-black-lives-matter.

Schriok, Stephanie. n.d. "EMILY'S List President: Trump Has Empowered American Women—by Accident." https://www.emilyslist.org/news/entry/emilys-list
-president-trump-has-empowered-american-women-by-accident.

Schwartz, Nancy. 2009. "Case Study: How a Nonprofit Name Change Generated
Attention and Momentum." https://web.archive.org/web/20090619094204/
http://www.nancyschwartz.com/nonprofit_name_change.html.

Scott, W. Richard. 2003. *Organizations: Rational, Natural, and Open Systems.*
Upper Saddle River, N.J.: Prentice Hall.

Shaiko, Ronald G. 1999. *Voices and Echoes for the Environment: Public Interest
Representation in the 1990s and Beyond.* New York: Columbia University Press.

Shelley, Martha. 2003. Interview by Kelly Anderson. Voices of Feminism Oral History Project. Sophia Smith Collection, Smith College, Northampton, Mass.
https://www.smith.edu/libraries/libs/ssc/vof/transcripts/Shelley.pdf.

Shriver, Thomas E., and Chris Messer. 2009. "Ideological Cleavages and Schism
in the Czech Environmental Movement." *Human Ecology Review* 16, no. 2:
161–71.

Singh, Jitendra V., and Charles J. Lumsden. 1990. "Theory and Research in Organizational Ecology." *Annual Review of Sociology* 16: 161–95.

Skocpol, Theda. 2004. "The Narrowing of Civic Life." *The American Prospect.*
May 17. http://prospect.org/article/narrowing-civic-life.

Skocpol, Theda, Marshall Ganz, and Ziad Munson. 2000. "A Nation of Organizers:
The Institutional Origins of Civic Voluntarism in the United States." *American
Political Science Review* 94, no. 3: 527–46. https://doi.org/10.2307/2585829.

Snow, David A., Sarah A. Soule, and Hanspeter Kriesi. 2008. *The Blackwell Com-
panion to Social Movements.* Hoboken, N.J.: John Wiley.

Soule, Sarah A., and Brayden G. King. 2008. "Competition and Resource Partitioning in Three Social Movement Industries." *American Journal of Sociology*
113, no. 6: 1568–1610. https://doi.org/10.1086/587152.

Springer, Kimberly. 2001. "The Interstitial Politics of Black Feminist Organizations." *Meridians* 1, no. 2: 155–91.

Springer, Kimberly. 2005. *Living for the Revolution: Black Feminist Organizations, 1968–1980.* Durham, N.C.: Duke University Press.

Staggenborg, Suzanne. 1988. "The Consequences of Professionalization and Formalization in the Pro-Choice Movement." *American Sociological Review* 53,
no. 4: 585–605. https://doi.org/10.2307/2095851.

Staggenborg, Suzanne. 1989. "Stability and Innovation in the Women's Movement: A Comparison of Two Movement Organizations." *Social Problems* 36,
no. 1: 75–92. https://doi.org/10.2307/800551.

Staggenborg, Suzanne. 1991. *The Pro-Choice Movement: Organization and Activism in the Abortion Conflict.* New York: Oxford University Press.

Staggenborg, Suzanne, and Verta Taylor. 2005. "Whatever Happened to the Women's Movement?" *Mobilization: An International Quarterly* 10, no. 1: 37–52. https://doi.org/10.17813/maiq.10.1.46245r7082613312.

Stefansky, Emma. n.d. "Women's March Dials Up Major Crowd Size Numbers across the U.S." *The Hive.* https://www.vanityfair.com/news/2018/01/womens-march-crowd-size-numbers.

Stein, Perry. 2017. "Protesters Plan March for Truth to Demand Independent Russia Investigation." *Washington Post.* June 1. https://www.washingtonpost.com/local/protesters-plan-march-for-truth-to-demand-independent-russia-investigation/2017/06/01/5da25ca4-4639-11e7-98cd-af64b4fe2dfc_story.html.

Stein, Perry, Michael Alison Chandler, and Sandhya Somashekhar. 2017. "The Strike Is On: Women Protest as Part of 'Day without a Woman.'" *Washington Post.* March 8. https://www.washingtonpost.com/local/the-strike-is-on-women-protest-as-part-of-day-without-a-woman/2017/03/08/f1da5ec8-0415-11e7-b1e9-a05d3c21f7cf_story.html.

Stockman, Farah. 2017. "Women's March on Washington Opens Contentious Dialogues about Race." *New York Times.* January 9. https://www.nytimes.com/2017/01/09/us/womens-march-on-washington-opens-contentious-dialogues-about-race.html.

Stryker, Sheldon. 2000. "Identity Competition: Key to Differential Social Movement Participation?" In *Self, Identity, and Social Movements,* edited by Sheldon Stryker, Timothy Joseph Owens, and Robert W. White, 21–40. Minneapolis: University of Minnesota Press.

Suchman, Mark C. 1995. "Managing Legitimacy: Strategic and Institutional Approaches." *Academy of Management Review* 20, no. 3: 571–610. https://doi.org/10.2307/258788.

Tarrow, Sidney G. 1998. *Power in Movement: Social Movements and Contentious Politics.* New York: Cambridge University Press.

Time. 1975. "The Sexes: Womenswar." December 1.

Tolentino, Jia. 2017. "The Somehow Controversial Women's March on Washington." *The New Yorker.* January 18. http://www.newyorker.com/culture/jia-tolentino/the-somehow-controversial-womens-march-on-washington.

Toni Carabillo and Judith Meuli Papers. 1991. "Chronology of the Split." MC 725, folder 29.15–29.16. Schlesinger Library, Radcliffe Institute, Harvard University, Cambridge, Mass.

Touré. 2017. "A Year Inside the Black Lives Matter Movement." *Rolling Stone.* December 7. https://www.rollingstone.com/politics/news/toure-inside-black-lives-matter-w513190.

Tully, Mary Jean. 1992. Interview by Mary Jean Collins. Tully–Crenshaw Feminist Oral History Project Records, 1961–2001. MC 548, folder 6.10–7.1. Schlesinger Library, Radcliffe Institute, Harvard University, Cambridge, Mass.

Turk, Katherine. 2010. "Out of the Revolution, into the Mainstream: Employment Activism in the NOW Sears Campaign and the Growing Pains of Liberal Feminism." *Journal of American History* 97, no. 2: 399–423.

Waddell, Kaveh. 2017. "The Exhausting Work of Tallying America's Largest Protest." *The Atlantic.* January 23. https://www.theatlantic.com/technology/archive/2017/01/womens-march-protest-count/514166/.

Walker, Edward T., and John D. McCarthy. 2010. "Legitimacy, Strategy, and Resources in the Survival of Community-Based Organizations." *Social Problems* 57, no. 3: 315–40. https://doi.org/10.1525/sp.2010.57.3.315.

Walker, Edward T., John D. McCarthy, and Frank Baumgartner. 2011. "Replacing Members with Managers? Mutualism among Membership and Nonmembership Advocacy Organizations in the United States." *American Journal of Sociology* 116, no. 4: 1284–1337. https://doi.org/10.1086/655753.

Walters, Daniel. n.d. "After the 2018 Spokane Women's March Was Suddenly Canceled, Activists Scrambled to Resurrect It." *Inlander.* https://www.inlander.com/Bloglander/archives/2018/01/05/after-the-2018-spokane-womens-march-was-suddenly-canceled-activists-scrambled-to-resurrect-it.

Wang, Dan J., and Sarah A. Soule. 2012. "Social Movement Organizational Collaboration: Networks of Learning and the Diffusion of Protest Tactics, 1960–1995." *American Journal of Sociology* 117, no. 6: 1674–1722. https://doi.org/10.1086/664685.

Ware, Gilbert. 1994. "The NAACP-Inc. Fund Alliance: Its Strategy, Power, and Destruction." *Journal of Negro Education* 63, no. 3: 323–35. https://doi.org/10.2307/2967184.

WBUR. n.d. "One Scholar on the Future of Black Lives Matter." http://www.wbur.org/hereandnow/2017/04/05/peniel-joseph-black-lives-matter.

Weber, Klaus, and Daniel Waeger. 2017. "Organizations as Polities: An Open Systems Perspective." *Academy of Management Annals* 11, no. 2: 886–918. https://doi.org/10.5465/annals.2015.0152.

Weber, Max. 1998. *From Max Weber: Essays in Sociology.* New York: Routledge.

Wehr, Paul. 1986. "Nuclear Pacifism as Collective Action." *Journal of Peace Research* 23, no. 2: 103–13. https://doi.org/10.1177/002234338602300202.

Whittier, Nancy. 1997. "Political Generations, Micro-Cohorts, and the Transformation of Social Movements." *American Sociological Review* 62, no. 5: 760–78. https://doi.org/10.2307/2657359.

Whittier, Nancy. 2006. "From the Second to the Third Wave: Continuity and Change in Grassroots Feminism." In *The U.S. Women's Movement in Global Perspective,* edited by Lee Ann Banaszak, 45–67. Lanham, Md.: Rowman and Littlefield.

Withey, Michael J., and William H. Cooper. 1989. "Predicting Exit, Voice, Loyalty, and Neglect." *Administrative Science Quarterly* 34, no. 4: 521–39. https://doi.org/10.2307/2393565.

Witt, Emily. 2018. "How the Kavanaugh Nomination Has Intensified the Feminist Protest Movement." *The New Yorker,* September 26. https://www.newyorker.com/news/news-desk/how-the-kavanaugh-nomination-has-intensified-the-feminist-protest-movement.

Women's Equity Action League Records. 1967a. "Dear N.O.W. Member, December 27." MC 311, folder 1.27. Schlesinger Library, Radcliffe Institute, Harvard University, Cambridge, Mass.

Women's Equity Action League Records. 1967b. "Thoughts for Organization by Betty Boyer." MC 311, folder 1.27. Schlesinger Library, Radcliffe Institute, Harvard University, Cambridge, Mass.

Women's Equity Action League Records. 1968. "Dear Phineas, February 12." MC 500, folder 1.27. Schlesinger Library, Radcliffe Institute, Harvard University, Cambridge, Mass.

Women's Equity Action League Records. 1976. "To Prof. Eric Goldman From Bernice Sandler, February 25." MC 500, folder 1.31. Schlesinger Library, Radcliffe Institute, Harvard University, Cambridge, Mass.

Women's March. 2017. "Power to the Polls." https://www.womensmarch.com/power-to-the-polls/.

Women's March on Portland. 2018. "This is a last warning. [T]his group will be shutting down this coming Wednesday at noon . . ." Facebook, January 8. https://www.facebook.com/groups/WomensMarchOnPortland/.

Worthen, Meredith G. F. 2014. "Blaming the Jocks and the Greeks? Exploring Collegiate Athletes' and Fraternity/Sorority Members' Attitudes toward LGBT Individuals." *Journal of College Student Development* 55, no. 2: 168–95. https://doi.org/10.1353/csd.2014.0020.

Wrenn, Corey Lee. n.d. "Professionalization, Factionalism, and Social Movement Success: A Case Study on NonHuman Animal Rights Mobilization." PhD diss., Colorado State University. https://dspace.library.colostate.edu/bitstream/handle/10217/173348/Wrenn_colostate_0053A_13455.pdf.

Yu, Kyoung-Hee. 2012. "Formal Organizations and Identity Groups in Social Movements." *Human Relations* 65, no. 6: 753–76. https://doi.org/10.1177/0018726712439908.

Zald, Mayer N., and Roberta Ash. 1966. "Social Movement Organizations: Growth, Decay and Change." *Social Forces* 44, no. 3: 327–41. https://doi.org/10.1093/sf/44.3.327.

Zald, Mayer N., and Michael A. Berger. 1978. "Social Movements in Organizations: Coup d'Etat, Insurgency, and Mass Movements." *American Journal of Sociology* 83, no. 4: 823–61.

Zald, Mayer N., and John D. McCarthy. 1980. "Social Movement Industries: Competition and Cooperation among Movement Organizations." *Research in Social Movements, Conflicts, and Change* 3: 1–20.

Zald, Mayer N., Calvin Morrill, and Hayagreeva Rao. 2005. "The Impact of

Social Movements on Organizations: Environment and Responses." In *Social Movements and Organization Theory,* edited by Gerald F. Davis, Doug McAdam, W. Richard Scott, and Mayer N. Zald, 253–79. New York: Cambridge University Press.

Zernike, Kate. 2018. "Working to Ensure the 'Year of the Woman' Is More Than Just One Year." *New York Times.* December 10. https://www.nytimes.com/2018/12/10/us/politics/women-candidates-activism.html

KELSY KRETSCHMER is assistant professor of sociology at Oregon State University.